PETER HOLMAN

LEEDS BAROQUE
PROGRAMME NOTES
2000-2018

978-1-912271-39-9

List of Subscribers

Richard & Gillian	Andrews	Patricia	McClelland
Olav & Liz	Arnold	Felicia	McCormick
Eboracum	Baroque	Michael	McGlashan
Clifford	Beddows	Peter	Meredith
Gill	Bracey	Dan	Merrick
Tony	Brigg	Sue	Mottram
Roger William	Brock	Stephen	Muir
Kirsty	Bullen	Leslie	Naylor
Clare	Bussingham	Victoria	Nicholls
Catherine	Carr	Michael	O'Donnell
Ann	Christys	Anthony	Ogus
Shirley	Clarkson	Alan & Caroline	Pearman
Ann	Crabtree	Nina	Platts
Ben	Cunliffe	Alan & Pam	Radford
Tim & Alison	Down	Patricia	Ralls
Robert	Drewett	Richard	Rastall
Clare	Druce	Derek	Revill
Gill	Eastabrook	Terry	Riley
Emma	Edgar	Richard	Robbins
Kathleen Margaret	Evans	Stephen	Robinson
Joanne	Fairley	Gillian M	Roche
Simon	Feather	Peter A	Rose
David	Forsdike	Joanna	Rowling
Jo	Green	K	Rundell
Michael	Green	Julian	Rushton
Philip	Gruar	Heather	Sager
Jenny	Hakney	Adrian	Salmon
Gregory	Halbe	Nicki	Sapiro
Jennifer	Hardy	Graham	Smith
Catherine	Haworth	Marjorie	Smith
Graham	Hill	Michael Arthur	Smith
Peter	Holman	Philip	Smith
Robert	Holt	M	Srivastava
Kathy	Hoole	Martin	Staniforth
David A	Jackson	Bradley	Studd
Louise	Jameson	Judy	Tarling
Alan	Jarvis	Cheryl	Thorne
Christopher & Jillian	Johnson	Delma	Tomlin
Alan & Amanda	Kelly	Dave	West
George	Kennaway	Jo	Wherry
Gill	Knowles	Rachael	Wherry
Geoffrey & Joy	Lawrence	Bryan & Caroline	White
Marie	Lemaire	Eileen	White
Polly	Lusher	Perry	White
Thomas H	MacFarlane	Daniel	Yeadon
Carola	Maddox		
Susan	Marshall		

And twenty anonymous donors

CONTENTS

	Page
Acknowledgements	4
Foreword	5
Biography	6

J.S. Bach
    Mass in B minor   7
    Bach at Christmas   8
    Cantatas 'Non sa che sia dolore' and 'Ich habe genug'   9

C.P.E. Bach
    St Matthew Passion   10

J.C. Bach
    The Bach-Abel Concerts   11

Heinrich Biber
    Missa Sancti Henrici   14
    Peter Holman's Birthday Concert   16

G.F. Handel
    The *Messiah*   16
    Music for Court and State   17
    The Coronation Anthems   18
    Te deum and Jubilate for the Peace of Utrecht   19
    L'Allegro, il Penseroso ed il Moderato   20

Felix Mendelssohn
    The Lutheran Chorales   22

W.A. Mozart
    Coronation Mass K317   23

Henry Purcell
    King Arthur   24
    The Fairy Queen   26

Jean-Philippe Rameau
    A Portrait   27

Claudio Monteverdi
    Il ballo delle Ingrate   29

John Blow
    Venus and Adonis   29

Vivaldi and Pergolesi
    Kyrie and Gloria   30
    Missa di San Emidio[1]

Various
    Concert Spirituel: Music at The French Court   33
    Made in the North: Provincial Music in the
    North of England in the Eighteenth and Nineteenth Centuries   35
    The Baroque Concerto: Corelli, Vivaldi and Handel   37

Appendix
    Leeds Baroque repertoire 2000- 2018   38

Acknowledgements

Our thanks are due to all who have helped in the production of this book and particularly to:

    Peter Holman for providing the inspiration for the collection.

    Ruth and Jeremy Burbidge and their team at Peacock Press for their invaluable advice on book production.

    Dan Merrick for sowing the seed of the Timpani project.

    Adrian Bending for his advice on the purchase of instruments and his generosity in lending his set to us whilst the project was developed.

    Louise Goodwin for providing the 'friendly face' of timpani and brilliant percussion skills.

    The proof reading team and last but not least all those who supported the project through the crowdfunding campaign or purchasing this book.

---

[1] Programme Note by Andrew Wooley

Foreword: Sir Alan Langlands

I am delighted to introduce this collection of programme notes, produced as part of the Baroque Timpani project and Leeds Baroque's twentieth anniversary celebrations.

Thank you all for your contributions to this exciting project – every penny will make a huge difference to Leeds Baroque, and we hope that other groups in Yorkshire will also use the timpani from time to time, adding greatly to the range, depth and interest of their work.

One of the many things I enjoy about Leeds Baroque performances is Peter Holman's direction of the ensemble from the harpsichord. Apparently without effort, he inspires coherence, togetherness and a great spirit in the group, blending the sound of the instruments and voices in a magical way. This is a largely voluntary ensemble with a truly professional attitude. The strength of their commitment is always evident in the warmth of their performances, which combine the enthusiasm of people giving up their own time to perform, with the detail, discipline and precision characteristic of professional music making.

Leeds Baroque performances have an intimacy of sound and ambience; they give me a sense of being transported to another age, perhaps relaxing in a seventeenth or eighteenth century salon! There is also something in the visual impact, in the sound and in the atmosphere of their performances that makes the whole experience special. This is always enhanced by the context provided in the Peter's fascinating programme notes, meticulously prepared for each concert.

Leeds Baroque adds to the great diversity of the cultural offer in Leeds, and it makes a truly distinctive contribution. I know from personal experience that audiences across the age range value its performances, including many of the University's staff and students from home and abroad.

Alan Langlands

Peter Holman

Peter Holman
Director – Leeds Baroque

Peter Holman studied at King's College, London with Thurston Dart, and founded the pioneering early music group Ars Nova while a student. He is now director of The Parley of Instruments and the choir Psalmody, is musical director of Leeds Baroque and director of the annual Suffolk Villages Festival.

Peter has taught at many conservatories, universities, and summer schools in Britain, Europe and the USA. He was appointed Reader in Historical Musicology at Leeds University of Leeds in January 2000, retiring as Emeritus Professor in 2010.

He is a regular broadcaster on BBC Radio 3, and is much in demand as a lecturer at learned conferences. He spends much of his time in writing and research, and has special interests in the early history of the violin family, in instrumental ensemble music of the Renaissance and Baroque, and in English music from about 1550 to 1850. He is the author of the prize-winning book *Four and Twenty Fiddlers: The Violin at the English Court 1540-1690* (Oxford, 1993), a much-praised study of Purcell's music (Oxford, 1994), a book in the Cambridge Music Handbook series on Dowland's *Lachrimae* (Cambridge, 1999) and *Life after Death: The Viola da Gamba in Britain from Purcell to Dolmetsch*.

In 2015 Peter was awarded an MBE for services to music in the New Year Honours list. He is writing a study of conducting and musical direction in Georgian Britain entitled *Before the Baton*.

Leeds Baroque Registered Charity No.1116610

Leeds Baroque is a period instrument performance group (choir and orchestra) based in West Yorkshire directed by Peter Holman. Members are drawn from professional and non-professional players with students from the University of Leeds School of Music and the region's music colleges and conservatoires. Free workshops given by leaders in the field of Baroque performance practice provide training, and the funds available are used to enable members of the orchestra to perform concerts with internationally renowned soloists. Both the choir and orchestra have launched several young performers on their professional careers.

Their repertoire is wide ranging, encompassing great Baroque 'standards' such as Bach, Handel and Purcell but including less frequently performed works by composers of the period. Leeds Baroque is a regular contributor to the University of Leeds International Concert series (http//:concerts.leeds.ac.uk) and in 2015 was delighted when the Vice Chancellor of the University, Sir Alan Langlands, accepted an invitation to become their Honorary Patron.

Leeds Baroque is supported by a grant from Wades Charity and an active and lively Friends organisation that provides both financial and practical assistance. The Friends have helped in the purchase of instruments for use by up-and-coming students and they frequently provide grants to cover professional fees of guest artists and the hire of performance material. Their support is greatly valued and allows Leeds Baroque to be more adventurous in its programming.

PROGRAMME NOTES

J.S. Bach (1685-1750)
Mass in B Minor

The B Minor Mass is arguably Bach's greatest single work. It is one of the longest settings of the Ordinary of the Mass – the fixed sequence of 'Kyrie', 'Gloria', 'Credo', 'Sanctus' and 'Agnus Dei' – said or sung, every time a Roman Catholic mass is celebrated. The compilation of the complete mass also seems to have been Bach's last compositional project, perhaps completed in 1749, the year before his death and after he stopped work on the Art of Fugue, which has traditionally been thought of as his last work.

We are so accustomed to the idea that the B Minor Mass is a single monumental work that it comes as a shock to realise that it is a compilation, made up of music written over a 35-year period.

The earliest complete portion is undoubtedly the 'Sanctus', written as a separate work for performance in Leipzig on Christmas Day 1724. Next comes the so-called Missa, the 'Kyrie and Gloria' (the two movements normally found in the Lutheran liturgy of the period), which seems to have been written for performance at the Dresden court in 1733. The other movements, the 'Credo' and the final sequence of 'Osanna, Benedictus, Agnus Dei and Dona nobis pacem', were apparently put together when the whole mass was compiled, in 1748-1749, though they contain music that is known or suspected to have been adapted from earlier works. The earliest that has been identified is the 'Crucifixus' in the Credo, which is an adaptation of the first chorus of Cantata no. 12, *Weinen, Klagen, Sorgen, Zagen*, written in 1714. Other arrangements include the 'Et expecto', arranged from a chorus in Cantata no. 120, and the 'Agnus Dei', which is also an aria in the Ascension Oratorio, Cantata no. 11. When Bach wrote the Missa in 1733 he also used several existing movements. The 'Gratias agimus' in the Gloria (repeated as the 'Dona nobis pacem' at the end of the work) comes from the first chorus of Cantata no. 29, *Wir danken wir, Gott* of 1731, while the 'Qui tollis peccata mundi' is a shortened arrangement of the first chorus of Cantata no. 46 (1723). In some cases we can guess that the music is an arrangement even though the original does not survive. For instance, the 'Quoniam in the Gloria', scored for bass, horn, two bassoons and continuo, seems to have been arranged from a lost piece written an octave higher for alto, trumpet, two oboes and continuo.

If the B minor Mass draws upon music written over most of his mature composing career, it also uses an extraordinary variety of musical styles, ranging from the traditional contrapuntal techniques of the Renaissance to the latest operatic idioms. The Renaissance technique of deriving a contrapuntal movement from a slow-moving plainsong *cantus firmus* can be heard in the first movement of the 'Credo' and in the 'Confiteor', where the plainsong appears at several points in long notes in the tenor part. In other movements, such as the first 'Kyrie' and the 'Gratias agimus', the music is fugal but the writing is more modern, with independent writing for the instruments. The 'Crucifixus' uses another favourite Baroque musical device: it is a set of variations over a chromatic ground bass, essentially the same as the one in Dido's Lament from Purcell's *Dido and Aeneas*. Most of the other choruses use a more up to date style that mixes counterpoint, choral declamation and concerto-like writing for the instruments. The arias, particularly in the 'Gloria', are written in the fashionable operatic style popular at the Dresden court. This can be seen in, for instance, the use of the horn, a popular Dresden instrument, in the 'Quoniam', and the virtuoso writing for soprano and solo violin in the Laudamus te, with its elaborate ornamentation, and the 'Domine Deus' with its sighing appoggiaturas and its backward dotted rhythms – a feature of the modern *galant* style. Such diversity should be seen as an aspect of Bach's desire to produce a profound and universal masterpiece that summed up and referred to most of the musical traditions of his time.

Schlosskirche at Weimar

Bach at Christmas

In this programme, we bring together five works for the Christmas season written by (or associated with) Johann Sebastian Bach; they cover the period from Advent to the New Year. They range across most of his adult career, from the period in his twenties when he was court organist and Konzertmeister in Weimar at the court of Johann Ernst of Sachsen-Weimar, to his old age at St Thomas's Church in Leipzig, when he had more or less given up writing new church works and was mostly recycling his earlier music.

We begin with Cantata no. 61, *Nun komm der heiden Heiland*, composed in Weimer for Sunday, 2 December 1714. As befits a work written for the start of the Lutheran church year it begins with a movement that combines Martin Luther's great Advent chorale with the idiom of the French overture, used to preface large-scale works all over Europe at the time. Bach even uses French-style orchestral writing with a single violin part and two violas. After this there is a succession of recitatives and arias, including a striking recitative in which Jesus knocks on the door, illustrated by harsh harmony and pizzicato strings. The soul replies with an intimate aria accompanied just by violoncello and harpsichord. The work ends with a short, joyful setting of a fragment from Philip Nicolai's famous chorale *Wie schön leuchtet der Morgenstern*.

Next comes a short setting of the 'Sanctus' in Latin, written for Bach's first Christmas in Leipzig and first performed on 25 December 1723. It is a virtuoso showpiece for the choir, packing a great deal of dense, florid counterpoint into two brief sections. The orchestra largely doubles the vocal lines though the first violin part is independent, making a five-part texture.

The charming Christmas cantata *Es ist ein Kind geboren* was thought to be by J.S. Bach in the nineteenth century, and was later attributed to Johann Kuhnau, his predecessor at Leipzig, though the consensus at present is that it is not by him either. It is conventionally dated *c.*1720, though its rather simple, almost rustic idiom suggests a somewhat earlier date. Neumeister's text was published in 1711, and the cantata's up-to-date scoring, with obbligato Baroque recorders and oboes, probably means it was written around then. As was common at the time, the composer seems to use the wind instruments to represent two groups featured in the Christmas story: shepherds were conventionally represented by recorders while the oboes are probably meant to portray the town band of Bethlehem, playing around the crib. After the opening single-section 'Concerto' and the linked first chorus, the cantata mostly consists of a succession of arias accompanied by pairs of solo instruments. It ends with a concerted setting of the last verse of the chorale *Wir Christenleut haben jetzund Freud*.

The Mass in A major is one of four short Lutheran masses (consisting just of Kyrie and Gloria) that Bach compiled around 1740, apparently drawing mostly on earlier works. It includes movements he had already used in Cantatas nos. 67 (the opening sequence of the 'Gloria'), 179 (the soprano aria 'Qui tollis peccata mundi', 79 (the alto aria 'Quoniam tu solus sanctus') and 136 (the bulk of the 'Cum sancto spiritu' chorus), all written between 1723 and 1725. The four Lutheran masses have traditionally been neglected as mere compilations, though their musical quality is very high (Bach clearly chose some of his favourite and most memorable music for them), and of course his great Mass in B minor is also a compilation made along similar lines. There are several reasons for thinking that the Mass in A major was intended for Christmas. The key of A major was often used in the Baroque period for Christmas works, perhaps because the three sharps were thought to symbolise the Trinity, made manifest by the Incarnation, and by the 1730s the flute was often associated with Christmas, succeeding the obsolete recorder in that role. Also, the opening section of the 'Gloria' serves as a vivid depiction of a scene often portrayed by Renaissance artists. The angels hovering above the stable in Bethlehem sing praises in the vigorous choral sections, while the gentle solo sections featuring the flutes portray the rocking of the crib below.

Johann Sebastian Bach wrote his *Weichnachts-Oratorium* or Christmas Oratorio for the Christmas season at Leipzig in 1734-5. Despite its title, the work is not a conventional oratorio but a set of six cantatas designed to be performed on different days, beginning with the first cantata on Christmas day and concluding with the sixth on Epiphany, 6 January. Nevertheless, the cantatas have a number of features in common. As with his settings of the passion, they combine the Gospel narrative (sung mostly in recitative by the tenor soloist with a few choruses representing characters in the drama) with two layers of commentary. The chorales are drawn from the Lutheran hymn repertory of the sixteenth and seventeenth centuries. The arias, accompanied recitatives and introductory choruses are contemporary texts, probably by the Leipzig poet Christian Friedrich Henrici, who wrote under the pseudonym Picander. The fifth cantata, *Ehre sei dir, Gott, gesungen*, was first performed on 2 January and deals with the star leading the Magi to Bethlehem, Herod's response and the general theme of light brought to the world by the Incarnation. It is scored modestly but effectively with two oboes d'amore, strings and continuo, and begins with a joyful and captivating first chorus, thought to be adapted from a movement in a lost secular cantata.

Cantatas *Non sa che sia dolore* and *Ich habe genug*

The cantata *Non sa che sia dolore* is a puzzle. Its rather clumsy and muddled Italian text borrows lines from G.B. Guarini and Metastasio to mark the departure of someone connected with Ansbach. Scholars have suggested that the individual in question was Bach's friend J.M. Gesner, who came from near Ansbach and who left Leipzig in 1734 for the University of Göttingen. However, that does not explain why the text seems to be addressing someone who is leaving for military service overseas. There is little doubt, however, that the music is by Bach. It consists of a substantial sinfonia for flute and strings in the form of a da capo aria, followed by two recitatives and arias. The first aria is a large-scale and richly scored lament for the departure of the voyager with an elaborate flute obbligato, while in the delightful minuet-like second aria the voyager has left all his fears behind him.

The presentation at the Temple - Peter Paul Rubens

His cantata *Ich habe genug* was first performed on 2 February 1727. In this form it was scored for solo bass and oboe with strings and continuo. It was evidently one of his favourite works, surviving in at least five versions. The one we are performing this afternoon was probably produced in 1731. It is in E minor rather than C minor and is scored for a flute and soprano rather than oboe and bass voice. Later still he produced a version for alto and oboe, and two revised versions for bass voice. The work is an extended meditation on death, prompted by the scriptural reading for the Feast of the Purification, in which Simeon considered himself ready to die after seeing the infant Jesus in the temple. The first aria with its elaborate flute obbligato is a beautiful essay in world-weariness and longing for death, while the second is an affecting lullaby in rondo form with exquisite string writing. The work ends with a lively aria in minuet rhythm in which the singer joyfully embraces death.

C.P.E. Bach (1714-1788)
St Matthew Passion

In the spring of 1768 Carl Philipp Emanuel Bach, second son of Johann Sebastian Bach, succeeded Telemann as Musical Director of the city of Hamburg; Telemann, who had occupied the post for forty six years, had died the previous summer. One of the duties of the post was to compose an annual setting of the passion, to be performed in Hamburg's churches during Lent and Holy Week. By the time Bach had been released from his post at the Prussian court it was too late for him to write a passion for 1768, so Telemann's 1736 St Luke passion was revived. The following year, however, he chose to set the narrative in St Matthew's gospel, and the resulting work was performed a number of times between 5 February and 24 March, Good Friday. After these performances the 1769 St Matthew Passion was never revived by Bach, though material from it was used in a passion cantata he compiled in 1772. The full score and the set of performing parts eventually found their way with many of Bach's other choral works into the library of the Sing-Akademie in Berlin, where they remained until the Second World War. They were thought to have been destroyed during the war until 1999, when they were unexpectedly rediscovered in a library in Kiev. The work has been revived a number of times in continental Europe, and has even been recorded, though tonight's performance is almost certainly only the second ever in Britain.

In eighteenth-century Germany settings of the passion normally contained three elements: the gospel text was sung in recitative by the Evangelist and other singers taking the roles of Jesus and the other characters. The narrative was enriched by two layers of commentary: the chorales, which were mostly sixteenth- or seventeenth-century melodies and words, and the accompanied recitatives and arias, which were settings by the composer of recently or newly devised texts, often supplied by a local poet. In the case of the 1769 St Matthew Passion, they may have been provided by the Prussian female poet Anna Louisa Karsch. The work is much shorter than J.S. Bach's setting because the libretto begins later in the story, in the Garden of Gethsemane, and it ends with Jesus's death. Nevertheless, it was much longer than was the practice in Hamburg: C.P.E. Bach's later passion settings were required to last only about 45 minutes.

It was the rule at the time for passions to be *pasticcios* to a lesser or greater extent, using material from other settings of the passions or from other sacred works. Thus J.S. Bach's settings of the St Matthew and St John passions contain material from his other works. C.P.E. Bach almost certainly took part in one of the original performances of J.S. Bach's St Matthew Passion, and inherited a full score and a set of performance parts. For the 1769 passion he borrowed some of the crowd choruses from his father's setting (in the process reducing the double-choir writing to a single choir), as well as many of the chorales and some of the sections for the minor characters. At least one of the choruses was borrowed from elsewhere, from a setting of the passion by Gottfried August Homilius. In addition, the first chorus comes from his own setting of the Magnificat, written in 1749, while the last chorus, a setting of the German Kyrie, was borrowed from the 1725 setting of his father's St John Passion. However, the arias and accompanied recitatives were all newly composed, and are much more modern in style, adding horns in places, giving pairs of flutes and bassoons prominent obbligato parts, and using muted timpani to illustrate the earthquake after Jesus's death. Bach also responded to the enlightenment spirit of the words, which emphasise the personal relationship between Jesus and mankind, by using the modern 'sensibility style', with unexpected changes of musical direction, elaborate ornamentation and a frequent use of muted strings. The resulting work is quite different in mood and tone from that of his father's setting, but is an impressive work that deserves to become a regular part of the concert repertory.

The performing material used for today's performance is based on the critical edition *Carl Philipp Emanuel Bach: The Complete Works* (www.cpebach.org), and was made available by the publisher, the Packard Humanities Institute of Los Altos, California.

J. C. Bach (1735-1782)
C. F. Abel (1723-1787)
London Concert life in the Late Eighteenth Century

J. C. Bach

John (Johann) Christian Bach and Charles Frederick (Carl Friedrich) Abel were joint leaders of London's musical life for nearly 20 years. They went into partnership in 1765 to promote the concerts that bore their names, a venture that ended with Bach's death on 1 January 1782. They had known each other in Germany: J.S. Bach seems to have taught Abel in Leipzig around 1740, when J.C. Bach, his youngest son, was a child. Abel went to the Dresden court, eventually arriving in England in the winter of 1758-9, while J.C. Bach spent some years in Milan before coming to London in 1762. In addition to running the Bach-Abel concerts, which placed them at the head of the German faction among London's musicians, they worked as chamber musicians for Queen Charlotte, apparently composing a great deal of their chamber music for weekly concerts at Kew.

We do not know as much about the Bach-Abel concerts as might be expected from their fame because they were exclusive aristocratic subscription events that were never advertised in detail in the press. However, we know that they were initially organised in conjunction with the society hostess Theresa Cornelys at Carlisle House in Soho Square, moving to Almack's Assembly Rooms in
St James's in 1768, and then to the newly built Hanover Square Rooms in 1775. We know from eyewitnesses that, like other concerts at the time, they consisted of a mixture of symphonies and concertos, vocal music with orchestra, pieces for chamber ensemble and instrumental solos – hence the format for this afternoon's concert. Bach and Abel took turns directing the concerts, and a highlight of each one was Abel's viola da gamba solo. He was a gamba virtuoso first and foremost but also played the violoncello in the orchestra, and, like Bach, would have directed it from the harpsichord.

A large proportion of the orchestral pieces performed at their concerts were presumably by Bach and Abel themselves. They were largely responsible for popularising the *galant* style in England, which combined the simple, melodious style of up-to-date Italian opera with the rich orchestration of music written for the large German court orchestras. Bach's finest and most mature symphonies are in his op. 18 set, published shortly before his death. No. 4 in D major, with its brilliant scoring for flutes, oboes, bassoon, horns, trumpets and strings, was one of the most popular, and ideas from its driving first movement can be heard in a number of works by his contemporaries, including a symphony by Samuel Wesley and Mozart's Symphony no. 29.

Bach and Abel were dominant influences on the young Mozart. He was seven when he came to London with his father and sister in April 1764, and they stayed for more than a year, promoting public concerts and playing for the royal family and other private patrons. Most important for Wolfgang's development as a composer, while they were in London they were members of the Bach-Abel circle. He made a score of Abel's Symphony op. 7, no. 6 (which was why it was thought to be his Symphony no. 3 in the nineteenth century), and he wrote his first few symphonies in the same idiom. His Symphony no. 1 in E flat K16 was written in the autumn of 1764, possibly for a Bach-Abel concert, though it was probably also performed in the spring of 1765 in concerts promoted by his father. It is extraordinarily accomplished work for a child, with a taut and effective first movement, an Andante cleverly featuring cross rhythms and biting dissonances, and a rustic Rondo in the rhythm of a fast Italian minuet.

Carl Stamitz, a virtuoso violinist and viola player from Mannheim, spent several years in London in the late 1770s working in the Bach-Abel circle. Like Bach, he wrote many concertos or concerted symphonies in the Mannheim style featuring multiple soloists. The *Symphonia Concertante* in A major for violin, viola and violoncello uses the two-movement form popular at the time in London as well as in Mannheim: a large-scale Allegro is followed by a minuet in Rondo form. Mozart started to write a concerto in the same key for the same soloists in about 1779, evidently inspired by Stamitz's work, though he abandoned it in the middle of the first movement. This suggests that Stamitz wrote his own work while he was in London, perhaps for himself and other virtuoso players in the Bach-Abel concerts, though it was not published until 1784.

The vocal music sung in the Bach-Abel concerts included operatic arias as well as other songs with orchestra, and even settings of popular songs. Bach's beautiful settings of Scots songs (including 'The broom of Cowdenknows', scored for voice, two flutes, two violins and continuo) were published in the 1770s with the information that they had been sung at Hanover Square by the castrato Giusto Ferdinando Tenducci. Tenducci, who had spent some years working in Edinburgh, was famous for his performances of Scots songs. The two English songs in this afternoon's concert were published in collections of music for Vauxhall Gardens, though they too were probably first performed in the Bach-Abel concerts. In 'Cease awhile, ye winds, to blow', a delightful rondo in gavotte rhythm, the singer listens for her lover's voice as night comes on, to no effect. 'Midst silent shades and purling streams' begins as a Siciliana portraying Cupid inspiring love in 'deluded maids and swains', though the mood changes abruptly as he flies off in alarm, the full orchestra portraying 'the thunder of the war'. Abel's aria 'Frena le belle lagrime', his only major vocal work, was written for a production of the pasticcio opera *Sifari* at the King's Theatre in the Haymarket in 1767. Its eloquent viola da gamba obbligato portrays the emotions of the text, and incidentally gives us an idea of what his lost gamba concertos were like. The charming song 'When fond, you Damon's charms recite' by the Exeter composer William Jackson was not published until 1793 (it was the last gamba solo published in Britain before the late nineteenth century), though it may have been written much earlier for Abel. Jackson would have come into contact with him as a friend of the painter Thomas Gainsborough.

C. F. Abel

Abel's Quartet in G major is typical of the chamber ensemble pieces played in the Bach-Abel concerts. After going to one on 6 March 1765 Elizabeth Harris reported that she had heard 'a delightful quartetto' played by Abel, the violinist François-Hippolyte Barthélemon, the flautist Joseph Tacet and the cellist Giovanni Battista Cirri. The Quartet in G is Abel's only surviving work for flute, violin, gamba and violoncello, though his autograph score of a set of ten was advertised for sale after his death. Abel's Adagio in D minor gives us a good idea of how he might have improvised solo music on the viola da gamba, and shows us that his compositional range was far greater than is usually thought. Most of his instrumental music is in the elegant and charming *galant* style, but this one, with its florid ornamentation, richly chordal idiom and chromatic harmony, inhabits the tragic world of the gamba solos in J.S. Bach's passions or some of C.P.E. Bach's music in the *Empfindsamkeit* or sensibility style. Abel was sometimes compared at the time to the novelist Laurence Sterne, the foremost literary exponent of the cult of sensibility, at its height in the 1760s. One of his obituaries stated that "Sensibility is the prevailing and beautiful characteristic of his compositions.
– He was the *Sterne* of *Music*. – the one *wrote*, the other *composed* to the *soul*."

Heinrich Biber (1644-1704)
Missa Sancti Henrici

Heinrich Ignaz Franz Biber was born in Wartenberg (now Stráž pod Ralskem), near Reichenberg (now Liberec) in northern Bohemia. The son of a gamekeeper on the estates of Count Christoph Paul von Liechtenstein, he was employed as a young man by the Count's nephew, Karl Liechtenstein-Kastelkorn, Prince-Bishop of Olmütz (now Olomouc) at his court in nearby Kremsier (now Kroměříž) in central Moravia. We know virtually nothing about Biber's musical training, though the general assumption among scholars is that he studied in Vienna with the violinist and composer Johann Heinrich Schmelzer (c.1623-1680). His instrumental music takes its starting point from Schmelzer's works, and there are many points of contact between the two composers; Biber was a violinist first and foremost, though he also played the bass viol. In 1670 Biber moved to Salzburg as a musician in the employment of the prince-archbishop Maximilian Gandolph von Keunberg. He remained there for the rest of his life, rising through the ranks to become deputy Kapellmeister in 1679 and Kapellmeister in 1684; he was ennobled by the Austrian emperor in 1690, adding 'von Bibern' to his name. He died in Salzburg in 1704, where his house can still be seen, as well as a monument to him in the cemetery of St Peter's Abbey.

The main work in this afternoon's concert, the Missa *Sancti Henrici*, was written in 1696 for the ceremony in which his daughter Anna Magdalena was admitted to Nonnberg Abbey in Salzburg as a nun; she took the monastic name Maria Rosa Henrica after one of the abbey's patron saints, the Emperor Henry II – hence the name of the mass. It is scored for five-part voices and six-part strings with two trumpets and timpani (with three additional optional trumpets and trombones) and continuo. It exploits the contrasts between solo and tutti voices and strings; between sections in *stile antico* counterpoint (notably the 'Christe eleison' and the 'Qui tollis' section of the Gloria) and those in a more virtuoso, up-to-date style. It also contrasts the full sections and the intimate solos – notably the beautiful 'Et incarnatus' section of the Credo, scored for solo soprano and two violins without any bass instruments. The overriding impression left by the work is restraint and subtlety, as befits a work written in old age. It seems to have been Biber's last major work – his swansong – and it is fitting that its last movement, the 'Agnus Dei', is a masterclass in how to create a magical effect using elaborate counterpoint and cunningly placed shifting word accents.

I have planned the first half of the programme to present the Mass as it would have been heard in Salzburg in 1696, with instrumental music and motets interspersing its movements. For the offertory motet I have chosen a remarkable work, *In sole posuisti*, for solo soprano, solo violin and continuo. It survives anonymously at Kroměříž in a copy made by the composer Gottfried Finger (c.1655-1730), and so it has been attributed to him. However, Finger was a follower of Biber, and the work is more characteristic of the older composer, not least in the Alleluia section, a fine set of variations over a ground bass. For the communion motet I have chosen the *Litaniae Laurentanae* or Litany of Loreto, published in Biber's 1693 collection of Vesper music. As an extended prayer to the Virgin Mary, it would have been appropriate for the 1696 ceremony, and it is in similar in style to the mass, though without using trumpets and timpani. The Litany is always a test for a composer (only the best can cope with the repeated utterances of 'miserere nobis' and 'ora pro nobis' without inducing boredom!), a test Biber passes with flying colours.

The two sonatas from *Sonatae tam aris* in the first half of the programme are typical in that they consist of a number of short contrasted sections, sometimes with subtle links between them. We begin the concert with no. 12 in C major. It is scored for the full ensemble, two trumpets, six-part strings and continuo, and revels in rich eight-part textures, though it has a striking opening for the three violas alone. No. 10 is effectively a duet for trumpet and violin accompanied by two violas and continuo, and, most unusually for Baroque trumpet music, is in the minor; the trumpet part is written for a normal natural trumpet in C, exploiting notes in the harmonic series that can be applied to the key of G minor. This was a trick that Biber learned from Pavel Vejvanovský (the Kapellmeister at Kroměříž and a virtuoso trumpeter) who also wrote a sonata in G minor for the natural C trumpet. In the sonata Biber explores introspective emotions far removed from the martial heroics normally associated with the trumpet.

In the short second half of the programme we present four contrasted works for instrumental ensemble. The Partia (or suite) in A major for two *scordatura* violins and continuo comes from his last instrumental collection, *Harmonia artificiosa ariosa*, published in 1696. The tuning, a-e'-a'-e'', makes chords in the home key wonderfully sonorous – an effect particularly exploited in the opening movement. The final movement is particularly striking: a set of variations on the *ciacona* ground bass in which the violin parts are in strict canon. At one point Biber even manages to transfer the bass to the upper parts so that it is in counterpoint with itself, a contrapuntal tour de force also used by Henry Purcell.

The Battalia, written in 1673, is scored for a string ensemble in nine parts: three violins, four violas and two *violoni* (large bass violins or violoncellos) with continuo. It begins with a march-like introduction in which we seem to hear soldiers parading up and down and practising their fencing, illustrated by *col legno* bowing. Next comes the famous passage in which they sing drunkenly around the camp fire, each bawling out their own tune in a different key. After a short passage in which the soldiers practise their fencing again (this time illustrated by left-hand *pizzicato*), a military fife and drum strike up, portrayed respectively by the first violin and violone. A rustic dance-like interlude leads to a solemn aria, perhaps portraying 'serious thoughts before the battle'. Finally, the battle commences, illustrated by rapid musket fire in the upper parts and cannon in the basses. The last movement is a chromatic lament of the wounded musketeers.

The third sonata from *Sonatae tam aris* No. 7 in C major is mostly a set of variations over a ground bass in which the solo instruments, two trumpets and two violins, engage in a four-way conversation, formal, virtuosic and playful by turns. We end the concert with Biber's well-known Serenade in C major, also written in 1673. It is scored for five-part strings and continuo and is a conventional dance suite, with an Entrata, a melodious Allemanda and an Aria in the idiom of the *amener*, a lively triple-time dance derived from the branle. Then the string players put aside their bows and play a *ciacona* (the same ground bass as the one in the Partia in A major). During this the night-watchman appears and sings a traditional chorale, pointing out in the first verse that the church bell has struck nine and in the second (only a few seconds later!) that it has struck ten. Then follows a gavotte contrasting phrases played *arco* and *pizzicato*, and the suite ends with the Retirada, returning us to the mood of the opening.

Peter Holman's Birthday Concert

Heinrich Biber has been one of my favourite composers ever since I first heard recordings of some of his sonatas as a schoolboy, played by the pioneering Austrian period instrument group Concentus Musicus, directed by Nicolaus Harnoncourt. A little later, studying music in London, I rashly put on a concert containing a cross section of his instrumental works, including the work that ends this concert, the evocative Nightwatchman's *Serenade*. At that stage, in the late 1960s, Biber was known mainly as the composer of virtuoso and colourful solo violin music, particularly the remarkable cycle of fifteen Mystery or Rosary sonatas, which exploit the device of *scordatura*, the use of alternative tunings to alter the sonority of the violin and to facilitate the playing of chords in various keys. It was, therefore, a revelation to discover that Biber was also a master of larger-scale instrumental music. In 1983 I was privileged as a member of The Parley of Instruments to take part in the first complete recording of *Sonatae tam aris, quam aulis servientes* (1676), his first printed collection, which systematically explores varied combinations of two trumpets, two violins, three violas and continuo; three of them are included in this afternoon's programme. This collection shows that Biber did not depend just on virtuosity or on colourful programmatic effects (as in the celebrated Battalia): he was equally gifted as a melodist and as a master of counterpoint, with an acute ear for effective sonorities. Those virtues are also apparent in his church music, which has come to public attention in the last few decades as more of it has appeared in print. In 2000 I directed Leeds Baroque's performance of his monumental 53-part Missa Salisburgensis, written for Salzburg Cathedral in 1682 and requiring a minimum of about 75 performers, including 12 trumpets and two sets of timpani. After more than half a century listening to and performing Biber, I have come to the conclusion that he is one of the greatest composers of the seventeenth century, to rank with his contemporaries Marc-Antoine Charpentier in France and Henry Purcell in England. I hope you agree with me after hearing his concert.

G.F. Handel

G.F. Handel (1685-1759)
Messiah

Messiah occupies so central a place in our musical life that it comes as a shock to realise that the work is untypical of Handel's oratorios, and did not become popular until decades after his death. Its distinctive tone comes partly from Charles Jennens's superb libretto, which avoids direct narration, often alluding to the life of Christ indirectly through prophetic passages in the Old Testament. Musically, it is remarkable for its large number of choruses, and for the fact that a number of them are adapted from Italian duets, which gives them a light, chamber music quality. *Messiah* evolved as Handel adapted it during the 1740s to suit different soloists.

The version we are performing this afternoon is essentially the one that Handel had developed by the early 1750s. It has shortened versions of a number of the arias, which helps to keep the action moving and the length of the work within reasonable bounds. The one exception is the little-known version of 'How beautiful are the feet' as a duet for two altos with the chorus 'Break forth into joy'. Handel dropped the chorus after the first performances in Dublin, but revived it once in London in the 1750s. Leeds Baroque started its activities in 2000 with a performance of *Messiah*. It seemed a good idea to revisit the work now, using soloists drawn entirely from members of the choir past and present.

Queen Anne (1665 –1714)
Michael Dahl, 1705

Music for Court and State

This programme explores Handel's long and enduring relationship with the British state and with its royal family. The relationship began with the court ode 'Eternal source of light divine', written for Queen Anne's birthday on 6 February 1714, shortly after he had settled in London, and continued to the end of his composing career. We begin the concert with the *Anthem on the Peace*, Handel's last completed piece of church music; it was written to mark the Peace of Aachen and was performed in the Chapel Royal on 25 April 1749. It is rarely performed, presumably because it has been thought of merely as a compilation of movements from earlier works. Nevertheless Handel clearly went to a good deal of trouble to produce a distinctive and effective work, notable for its use of an obbligato flute and oboe in several movements. It begins with an ingenious reworking of the opening of the anthem 'As pants the hart' combined with the duet and chorus version of 'How beautiful are the feet', written for the original version of *Messiah* and later discarded. There follow a chorus first used in the Chapel Royal version of the anthem 'I will magnify thee' and a solo and chorus from *The Occasional Oratorio*, composed in 1746. The last chorus will also be familiar from *Messiah*, though it has a most unexpected ending.

The Concerto in D major is also rarely performed, mainly because the movements have not been recognised as belonging together and appear as three separate works in the catalogue of Handel's works and the related scholarly edition. It seems to have been composed in 1722 and may originally have been intended to be played in Act I of *Ottone*, though in the event only the sprightly second movement seems to have been used in the opera. To complicate matters, in 1734 John Walsh published this movement in the concerto grosso op. 3 no. 6 coupled with an unrelated organ concerto movement in D minor. The original four-movement version of the concerto deserves to be better known, not least for its slow movement, scored specifically for flute and solo violin with archlute continuo, and the vigorous final fugue, also used in the overture to *Ottone*.

The next piece, the short Italian solo cantata *Quel fior che all'alba ride*, also has connections with the royal family and with *Messiah*. It was written in about 1739, probably for Princess Louisa, the youngest daughter of George II. The theme of the last section will be familiar from the chorus *And he shall purify the sons of Levi*; there is an intermediate version in a movement of a duet on the same Italian text, composed in 1741, just before *Messiah*. Handel's song celebrating the Duke of Cumberland's victory over the Scots in 1745 is also little-known, presumably because it offends modern sensibilities and John Lockman's text is poor, though Handel produced a memorable swinging tune with a simple but effective orchestral accompaniment. If it seems familiar it is because a few years later, in 1749, Handel used several of the ideas in the second minuet of the Music for the Royal Fireworks.

1727 - George II official Coronation Medal

The Coronation Anthems

For the second half of the concert we turn from Handel rarities to his best-known anthems, written for the coronation of George II and Queen Caroline in Westminster Abbey on 11 October 1727. Handel was commissioned to write the anthems by the new king himself, over the head of Maurice Greene, who, as the recently appointed organist of the Chapel Royal, might have expected to have been chosen. Handel was evidently aware that too much loud triumphal music with trumpets and drums would be monotonous, so he took care to make the four anthems varied in style, with a number of quiet, almost reflective movements, notably in *My heart is inditing*, a suitably delicate anthem for the separate queen's coronation at the end of the service. *Zadok the priest* quickly became justifiably famous, and has been performed at every coronation since, prompted by William Boyce's refusal to reset the words for George III in 1760; Boyce remarked that "it cannot be more properly set than it has already been by Mr. Handel". As was usual with Handel, particularly when working at speed, he drew on a number of earlier works, even drawing on an early Italian psalm setting, *Nisi Dominus*, for the famous orchestral introduction to *Zadok the priest*.

Christopher Roberts – HANDEL *breath'd no more* Commissioned by Leeds Baroque 2015.

HANDEL *breath'd no more* is a four-movement ode based on an extract from The Tears of Music: A Poem to the Memory of Mr Handel by the Reverend John Langhorne of Hackthorne, Lincolnshire (dated 18 February 1760 and printed in *The Gentleman's Magazine*). The work uses the instruments and distinct sounds available to Handel and is scored for a period orchestra of trumpet, two oboes, bassoon with saprano, alto, tenor and bass vocal soloists, SATB choir, strings and continuo. Although written in a contemporary idiom, the work utilises historically-informed performance techniques, including bowing, articulation and phrasing. The ode opens with an orchestral symphony with concerto-grosso effects followed by a short accompanied recitative for bass soloist. The third movement, a slow homophonic chorus with short interjections by solo singers, leads immediately into a faster polyphonic chorus with French Baroque style notes *inégales*[2].

With special thanks to Leeds Inspired and Leeds Baroque Choir and Orchestra.
Christopher Roberts November 2015

[2] notes performed in a relaxed, swung rhythm though notated as equal in the score.

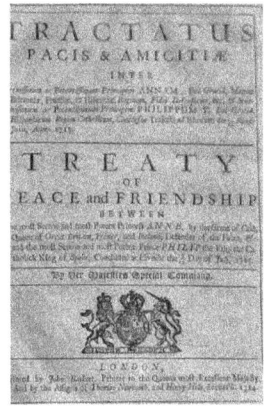

Te Deum and Jubilate for the Peace of Utrecht

The Treaty of Utrecht, which brought hostilities between France and Britain to a close following the War of the Spanish Succession, was signed in the Dutch city on 11 April 1713. In its provisions Britain acquired a number of overseas territories, including Newfoundland and Nova Scotia from France and Gibraltar from Spain – a bone of contention between the two countries up to the present. Another legacy was a number of musical works composed to celebrate the peace, three of which are performed in this afternoon's concert.

The main celebration was a service at St Paul's Cathedral on Tuesday, 7 July as part of a day of national rejoicing. It included the first performance of Handel's *Te Deum* and *Jubilate* in D major, as well as an anthem by William Croft for choir and organ. The 'Utrecht' Te Deum and Jubilate were composed in January and February 1713, presumably in anticipation of the signing of the treaty, and were rehearsed several times in March. They were Handel's first large-scale settings of English words, and belong to a tradition of English orchestral settings of the 'Te Deum' and 'Jubilate' initiated by Henry Purcell in 1694 and subsequently contributed to by John Blow, William Turner, Thomas Tudway and William Croft – whose 1709 'Te Deum' to celebrate the Battle of Malplaquet was probably Handel's immediate model. Handel's setting follows the earlier settings in that the 'Te Deum', with a lot of text to get through, moves briskly through the words in a kaleidoscopic patchwork of short, contrasted sections, with the emphasis on the choir and verse passages for multiple soloists rather than extended sections for one or two solo voices. The 'Jubilate' is a much shorter text than the 'Te Deum', so it allowed Handel to expand the size of his movements, and to demand more virtuosity from his vocal and instrumental soloists. The 'Jubilate' was composed about a month later than the Te Deum, so it may be that by then Handel had a better idea of the capabilities of his potential soloists. The Utrecht 'Te Deum' is the earliest choral work by Handel that remained in the repertory later in the eighteenth century. It was performed in St Paul's during the annual Festival of the Sons of the Clergy every other year (alternating with Purcell's settings) until 1743, when it was replaced by Handel's *Dettingen Te Deum*. The Dettingen setting is more spacious in its conception and more varied in its material than the earlier settings. Indeed, it is particularly attractive because it is so varied: it ranges through F sharp minor, A minor, F major, D minor, C major and G minor as well as the expected ceremonial D major, and a surprising amount of it explores introspective areas of feeling.

Soon after the service in St Paul's on 7 July William Croft (and doubtless a number of the members of the orchestra) set off for Oxford, where his ode 'With noise of cannon' was performed in the Sheldonian Theatre on 10 July along with a second Latin ode by Croft, *Laurus cruentas*. The occasion doubled as a delayed celebration of the Treaty of Utrecht and the Oxford Act, the occasional academic gathering for the conferring of higher degrees. Croft was receiving his D.Mus. in the company of the German composer Johann Christoph Pepusch, whose ode (now lost) was also performed. Croft's odes have texts by Joseph Trapp (1697-1747), a fellow of Wadham College, Oxford and the university's first Professor of Poetry. *From noise of cannon* is more old-fashioned than the Handel 'Te Deum and Jubilate', being in a post-Purcellian style, though it is none the worse for that. It begins with a splendid overture for trumpet and strings, consisting of a martial first movement (which Handel probably had in mind when he began to compose the fugue in the overture of his Fireworks Music), an elaborate double fugue, a short Adagio with expressive Purcellian harmonies, and a contrapuntal last movement in triple time. There follow a series of solos and duets for countertenor and baritone, some leading into choruses in the Purcellian manner. The last two movements, an expressive verse passage for six solo voices and orchestra and a triumphant final chorus with an extended fugue for all the voices and instruments, demonstrate Croft's ability to write in six parts – a requirement of the university regulations for the Oxford D.Mus. degree. We are grateful to Dr. Alan Howard for letting us use his edition of *With noise of cannon* for this performance.

The other work in this afternoon's concert, William Corbett's Suite in D major, comes at the end of his op. 3 sonatas, published in 1708. It is an extended work in the mixed French, Italian and English orchestral style as developed by Henry Purcell and his followers, with Italianate trumpet writing, a sequence of French-influenced dances, but also English – or rather British – idioms, including two movements in the 'Scotch' style popular in London at the time. Corbett was no Purcell, but he was capable of writing most attractive, tuneful music, with a feeling for string sonorities; he was an outstanding violinist and at the time was one of the leading players in the Italian opera orchestra at the Haymarket Theatre.

John Milton – poet
(1608 – 1674)

L'Allegro, il Penseroso ed il Moderato

When Handel wrote *L'Allegro, il Penseroso ed il Moderato* he had been living in England for nearly 20 years. He had originally come to London in 1710 to put on his opera *Rinaldo*, and for most of that time he had been preoccupied with Italian opera. However, during the 1730s he gradually discovered the creative and commercial potential of English texts. In the process, he invented a new genre, the English oratorio. Some of the English texts he set during this time were Biblical dramas such as *Athalia* and *Saul* - works that relate to some extent to the seventeenth-century Italian oratorio. Others, however, are secular rather than sacred, and relate more to the English choral tradition established by Purcell and his contemporaries with the annual odes on St Cecilia's day. For instance, Handel's *Alexander's Feast* (1736) and his *Ode on St Cecilia's Day* (1739) are settings of words by John Dryden originally written for the St Cecilia celebrations of 1697 and 1687 respectively.

In setting Dryden in the 1730s, Handel was responding to a wider interest in the past that was developing in England at the time. It was an early manifestation of Romanticism and went hand in hand with such things as a new interest in Shakespeare, with the revival of interest in Gothic architecture and with the development of antiquarian scholarship in all fields. In music, a landmark was Thomas Arne's 1738 setting of an adaptation of John Milton's masque *Comus*, originally performed in 1634. *Comus* was an enormous success, and part of the reason was that Thomas Arne's light, almost *galant* musical style was the perfect vehicle for Milton's rapturous evocations of nature. Handel clearly knew *Comus* and made good use of Arne's innovations when he came to write his own setting of Milton two years later.

Ironically, he found himself writing his setting of Milton's greatest evocation of the English countryside, *L'Allegro, il Penseroso ed il Moderato*, at the beginning of 1740, during the hardest winter in living memory, when few can have been thinking about the great outdoors.

Milton's twin poems *L'Allegro* and *Il Penseroso* develop themes used by Petrarch in several of his sonnets. Thus they are related to the anonymous sonnets inspired by Petrarch that Vivaldi used as the inspiration for his Four Seasons. In Milton's odes the characters Allegro and Penseroso exemplify what we would think of as extrovert and introvert personalities, and the delights of the natural world and human society are seen through their eyes. Thus Penseroso naturally prefers night, solitude and a hermit's cell while Allegro enjoys the bustle of cities and social pursuits such as dancing, hunting and the theatre. The original poems are separate, complementary works, but Handel's librettist Charles Jennens, developing a draft libretto written by the philosopher and prominent Handel supporter James Harris, saw the dramatic potential of juxtaposing lines from them in the first two parts of the work. Jennens wrote his own conclusion, the third part *Il Moderato*, expressing the virtues of moderation - a highly suitable text for the rationalist, enlightenment temper of the times. Indeed, the beautiful duet near the end is virtually an enlightenment credo, with its talk of 'rising reason' restoring 'intellectual day' by dispelling the fumes of superstition that had infected the mind. Jennens's contribution has been much mocked in modem times, for he was no Milton, though it is difficult to see how else the work could have been concluded, for the two states of mind are ultimately complementary. Elements of both are needed for a balanced personality, and thus one cannot be seen to triumph over the other.

L'Allegro, il Penseroso ed il Moderato has never been one of Handel's more popular oratorios, probably because it does not have the superficial attraction of a dramatic narrative, though by common consent it contains some of his finest music. At the age of 55 he was at the height of his powers; his next major work in English was to be his supreme masterpiece, *Messiah*. Handel responded with an astonishingly vivid imagination to Milton's nature pictures. He used a large orchestra and revelled in pictorial possibilities offered by it, writing for instance with exuberant virtuosity for the flute and the voice in *Sweet bird*, or finding in *Oft, on a plat of rising ground* exactly the right sound for a distant tolling bell - cellos and basses pizzicato with harpsichord left hand. But some of the most evocative music is devoted to illustrating less obviously pictorial ideas. For instance, the folk-like simplicity of *Let me wander, not unseen* is exactly right for Milton's breezy text, while in *Hide me from day's garish eye* he created an extraordinary atmosphere of dream-like softness, with music that often sounds almost out of its time. Such things testify to the hold England and the English scene had on our greatest immigrant composer.

We are performing *L'Allegro, Il Penseroso ed il Moderato* today essentially as first composed by Handel for the premiere, at the Lincoln's Inn Fields theatre in London on 27 February 1740; he made a number of changes to the work for later revivals, in 1741 and 1743. Handel gave all the music for Penseroso to a single soprano, to depict her solitary nature, but divided the Allegro music between a soprano (originally a boy treble), a tenor and a bass, portraying them collectively as a sociable being. We have increased the disparity between the two characters by further dividing up the Allegro soprano solos between three student members of the choir. Handel did not provide *L'Allegro* with an overture, instead using one of his newly composed op. 6 concertos; we have chosen the first movement of the G minor concerto, op. 6, no. 6, as an apt introduction to the first words, *Hence, loathed Melancholy*.

Felix Mendelssohn (1809-1847)
The Lutheran Chorales

Felix Mendelssohn came from a wealthy and highly cultured Jewish family in Hamburg: his grandfather Moses was a leading Enlightenment philosopher while his father Abraham was a successful member of the family bank. When Felix was two, in 1811, the family was forced to move to Berlin to escape the French occupation of Hamburg (the Mendelssohn bank had been financing Napoleon's opponents), and in 1816 his assimilation into Berlin society was facilitated when he and his three siblings were baptised into the Lutheran church. Living in Berlin enabled him to study composition with Carl Friedrich Zelter (1758-1832), the director of the Berlin Singakademie, the concert-giving organisation that had been founded in 1791 to perform old music, and specifically the music of J.S. Bach. Mendelssohn also came into contact with Bach's music through his aunt Sara Levy, who had been a pupil of Bach's eldest son Wilhelm Friedemann and a friend of his second son Carl Philipp Emanuel. Sara and Mendelssohn's father both acquired important collections of manuscripts of J.S. Bach's music, which were later acquired by the Singakademie. Mendelssohn experienced Bach's music in performance as a member of the choir and orchestra of the Singakademie, and in 1829 he conducted the organisation in a performance of the St Matthew Passion, the first outside Leipzig and a landmark in the Bach revival and the developing early music movement; he had received a score of the work from his grandmother Bella Salomon in 1823.

It is not surprising, therefore, that a number of Mendelssohn's early works are settings of Lutheran chorales in a style derived from Bach. The earliest of the three we are performing this afternoon is his setting of *Christe, du Lamm Gottes*, Martin Luther's metrical version of the 'Agnus Dei', scored for choir, strings and organ continuo. It was written in 1827 and was the first of Mendelssohn's Bach-inspired works. The published edition is based on two manuscripts in German libraries, but while we were preparing this concert we discovered that his autograph manuscript is in the Brotherton Library, at Leeds University; we are grateful to Joe Whelan for making a new edition of the piece from it for this afternoon's performance. The three-fold statement of the 'Agnus Dei' suggested to Mendelssohn a simple aria-like scheme, in which a flowing andante encloses a vigorous chromatic fugue. In all three sections the chorale tune is in slow notes in the soprano part with faster counterpoint in the lower parts, in time-honoured fashion, though Mendelssohn differs from Bach and his contemporaries in that the strings rarely double the voices, so much of the writing is in eight real parts.

Next in date of composition comes *Wer nur den lieben Gott la t walten*, a setting of a chorale by the seventeenth-century poet and musician Georg Neumark. Mendelssohn wrote it in 1829, while he was working on the St Matthew Passion, using a more extended sectional structure approximating to the pattern used by Bach in his cantatas. As with *Christe, du Lamm Gottes*, it is scored for choir, strings and organ continuo, though there is a central aria for solo soprano. It begins with a simple setting of the chorale, followed by an elaborate chorale fantasia based on the tune largely in eight-part counterpoint. The charming minuet-like aria is also written in an approximation of the Baroque style, though with a few more modern harmonies. The work ends with another splendid chorale fantasia, though with the whole choir singing the melody in unison until the last few bars, when it bursts into harmony – a striking touch.

Aus tiefer Not schrei' ich zu dir, a setting of Luther's metrical version of the 'De profundis' (Psalm 130), was written a year later, in 1830; it was the only one of his youthful chorale cantatas he felt worthy of publication, in his op. 23. It has a similar structure to *Wer nur den lieben Gott lasst walten*, with chorale fantasias framing solo movements, though it is apparently scored just for voices and organ. For this performance we have added strings doubling some of the movements; Mendelssohn would have been familiar with the eighteenth-century tradition of performing Lutheran motets with doubling instruments.

As a foil to the often rather severe counterpoint of Mendelssohn's Lutheran works, we have included two settings of Latin texts in what we might call his Catholic manner. The best-known is the splendid eight-part setting of the *Ave Maria*, written around the same time as *Aus tiefer Not* and published side-by-side with it in his op. 23. At the time he wrote both pieces he was in Italy, revelling in the Catholic south and its music. It is generally performed today just with organ accompaniment, though this afternoon we are using the original ensemble accompaniment, strikingly scored for two clarinets in A, two bassoons, cello and double bass with organ continuo. Mendelssohn's setting of that other favourite Catholic Marian text, the *Salve Regina*, is the earliest piece in this afternoon's concert. It was written in 1824, when he was fifteen years old, and belongs to a tradition of setting of the work for solo soprano and strings that stretches back to Handel and Pergolesi by way of John Christian Bach and Schubert. It is cast conventionally enough in the form an aria in the Mozartian style of the late eighteenth century, though Mendelssohn's response to the text and his writing for the voice and strings is astonishingly sophisticated for a teenager.

Wolfgang Amadeus Mozart (1756-1791)
Coronation Mass K317

Mozart was born in Salzburg, where his father Leopold was a court musician, and lived there on and off until 1781, when he moved to Vienna to work as a freelance musician. From 1773 until 1777, when he left Salzburg to seek his fortune in Paris and then Mannheim, he was employed alongside his father at the Salzburg court; on his return in 1779 he took up a position as court organist and concert master. One of his duties in Salzburg was to write church music for the cathedral, and our concert today is largely concerned with this aspect of his work.

The best-known of his Salzburg church works is the so-called Coronation Mass K317. Its rich scoring with horns, trumpets and drums suggests that it was written for a festive occasion, and it was long thought that it was entitled 'Coronation' because it was written for the anniversary of the coronation of the miracle-working image of the Virgin at the pilgrimage church of Maria Plain near Salzburg. However, it is now thought to have been first performed at Easter 1779 in Salzburg Cathedral. The mass is grand in scale, rich in ideas and full of contrasts, but is relatively short. The Archbishop of Salzburg had decreed that masses on feast days should not last more than forty five minutes, including the necessary motets at the Offertory and the Communion and the sonata customarily performed between the Epistle and the Gospel – or in musical terms between the 'Gloria' and the 'Credo' of the mass. Mozart mostly relies on brief solo quartet passages to contrast with the choral sections, the only extended solo being the expressive 'Agnus Dei', a forerunner of *Dove sono* in *Le nozze di Figaro*.

For this afternoon's performance the Epistle sonata is the one, in C major K329, that Mozart apparently wrote for the Coronation Mass. It has the same rich scoring with oboes, horns, trumpets and drums, to which the organ adds extra colour, mostly impersonating a pair of orchestral flutes. For the offertory motet we have chosen the vigorous double-choir *Venite populi*, written in Salzburg in 1776 for an Ascension Day service, and for the Communion the famous *Exsultate jubilate* K165 for soprano and orchestra. Mozart originally wrote it as a showpiece for the castrato Venanzio Rauzzini in Milan in 1773, but he revised it in Salzburg in 1779, probably for mass on Trinity Sunday. The text was changed in places and flutes replaced oboes in the orchestra.

The main item in the second half of the concert is the rarely performed *Litaniae de venerabili altaris Sacramento* (Litany of the Sacrament of the Venerable Altar) K243, written in Salzburg in March 1776. It is the largest and grandest of Mozart's four litany settings and may have been written for a great procession in Salzburg Cathedral on Corpus Christi – hence the use of the Corpus Christi plainsong hymn *Pange lingua* as a soprano *cantus firmus* in the 'Viaticum' movement. Mozart sets the verses of the Litany as a mixture of choral movements and elaborate operatic solos, always setting the repeated cries of *Miserere nobis* ('Have mercy on us') to different music. The climax of the work is the elaborate fugue *Pignus future gloriae*, followed by the expressive 'Agnus Dei', a virtuoso soprano solo with delicate oboe, flute and violoncello solos.

To complete the concert we have chosen one of Mozart's most charming and original short orchestral words, the *Serenata Notturna* K239, written in Salzburg in January 1776. It is effectively a reinvention of the Baroque concerto grosso, with a solo group consisting of two violins, viola and 'Contrabasso' and an orchestra of strings (without double bass) and timpani. All three movements are full of ideas evoking Austrian popular music. It begins with a march in which the solo group seem often to be imitating a village band, followed by a stately minuet and trio. The concluding rondo in the style of a rustic dance is interrupted by an adagio passage in an antique style evoking Baroque string music which then leads to an irresistible quick-step march.

Henry Purcell (1659-1695)
King Arthur

King Arthur, Henry Purcell's second major work for the London theatres, was produced at the Dorset Garden theatre in May 1691. Like its predecessor *Dioclesian*, produced the previous year, it was a musical play in which speech and music were more or less equally balanced. John Dryden's play seems to have been originally written a few years earlier to celebrate the 25th anniversary of the Restoration of the monarchy in 1660, but Charles II died in 1685 before it could be finished, and it was shelved for the rest of the decade. The plot pays little attention to the familiar stories about King Arthur from Medieval romance. In place of Camelot and the Knights of the Round Table, Dryden tried to get back to a historical British king, concerned with defeating the invading Saxons and unifying his kingdom. Unfortunately, without the benefits of modern archaeology, he had little to go on, and his plot is almost entirely invention. He did, however, retain the traditional figure of the wizard Merlin, and gave him an evil Saxon counterpart, Osmond.

In *King Arthur*, like other musical plays or 'semi-operas' of the period, the main characters – King Arthur, the blind princess Emmeline, Merlin, the Saxon King Oswald and Osmond – were spoken parts. Like earlier court masques, the music was sung by a succession of minor characters who might reasonably be expected to sing. In Act I music is used to portray Saxon priests sacrificing their victims, and British soldiers celebrating their victory, while in Act II shepherds and shepherdesses entertain Emmeline with songs and dances. However the most important musical scenes were devoted to the supernatural, conjured up either by Merlin or Osmond. In Act II Grimbald, an evil spirit in the service of Osmond, tries to lure King Arthur and his companions astray, but is thwarted by the repentant spirit Philidel; Philidel and Grimbald are unusual in Restoration drama in that they sing as well as speak. In Act III, Osmond conjures up the Frost Scene as a means of seducing Emmeline; the masque shows a frozen country being warmed by the power of love. In Act IV King Arthur is again led astray by Osmond's magic; he encounters seductive sirens and then a group of nymphs and sylvans in an enchanted grove. Finally, when Arthur has finally defeated the Saxons in Act V, Merlin puts on a masque for a spectacular conjuring show designed to show the Britons and Saxons that they will eventually form one united people.

Purcell's score for *King Arthur* has always been one of his most popular works. It held the stage in some form or other until the 1840s, and is frequently revived in the concert hall today. This is not just because it has pieces of superb quality such as the Frost Scene, the Passacaglia in Act IV and 'Fairest isle' in Act V. In his text Dryden understood, unlike the anonymous hacks who produced the adaptations of *Dioclesian* and *The Fairy Queen*, that Purcell needed a series of varied situations to produce the necessary contrasts of mood and idiom in the music without distorting its relationship with the parent play.

By the end of Act III of *King Arthur* one has experienced the solemn yet urgent music of the Sacrifice Scene, with its wonderful plunge into the minor at the words *Die and reap the fruit of glory*; the heroics of *Come if you dare*, with its stirring battle music; the ethereal spirit music of *Hither this way*, with its remarkable double-choir effects; the rustic jollity of the shepherds' scene later in Act II, and the brilliance and fantasy of the Frost Scene.

For this afternoon's performance I have tried to get back as close as possible to the form of Purcell's score performed in the original 1691 production. There are good reasons for thinking that he originally wrote the work without trumpets, and that several of the numbers that feature them, such as the D major trumpet overture, the symphony that follows Aeolus's appearance in Act V, and the extended setting of 'St George', were added for revivals after his death. The trumpet overture – which duplicates the D minor overture – was borrowed from the court ode 'Arise my muse', while 'St George' with its obbligato trumpet parts is too late in style and is too poor to be genuine. It was presumably written in the early eighteenth century by one of Purcell's followers. For this performance Richard Andrews has produced a script that tells the story, helps us to understand how Purcell's music fits into Dryden's play, and gives us a flavour of Dryden's wonderful poetry without, I hope, making too long an afternoon.

The Fairy Queen

The Fairy Queen was the third of the extravagant musical plays or dramatic operas that Henry Purcell wrote for the London stage; it was first performed at the Dorset Garden theatre on 2 May 1692. It was much more expensive than the preceding semi-opera, *King Arthur*: 'the clothes, scenes, and musick' cost £3000 according to the court chronicler Narcissus Luttrell, and the theatre prompter John Downes wrote that "the Expences in setting it out being so great, the Company got very little by it". It is an anonymous adaptation of Shakespeare's *A Midsummer Night's Dream*, which means that it has attracted more attention in this century than Purcell's other semi-operas, though most productions have tried to combine the music (which does not set a line of Shakespeare) with portions of the original play. More recently, Roger Savage and others have argued forcefully that the 1692 version of the text is the appropriate vehicle for the music, and works well in its own terms.

As with Purcell's other dramatic operas, his contribution to *The Fairy Queen* is concentrated mainly in a series of musical scenes or masques, most of which are conjured up for the entertainment of Titania and Oberon, the queen and king of the fairies. In the first act Titania and the fairies are entertained by a drunken stuttering poet, who has strayed into the 'spot of fairy ground'. It has been suggested that the poet is a portrait of the stuttering poet Thomas D'Urfey, and that he may have written the text and even acted the role himself. Titania's fairies lead him in blindfolded with two silent companions, and torment him until he admits to being a poor scurvy poet. Purcell portrays the irrationality of drunkenness in the same way as he portrays madness – with sudden changes of rhythmic direction – though the music has a delightful lightness that tells us that the malady is as temporary as the tormentors are insubstantial. At the end the poets are laid to rest with a delicious series of false relations.

The musical scene in Act II is sung in fairyland ('a Prospect of Grottos, Arbors, and delightful Walks') as Titania prepares for sleep. It falls into two halves: an entertainment put on for her by the fairies, and an extended masque-like lullaby. In the first half Purcell paints an evocative musical landscape of the wood at night: a birdsong passage on a descending ground for two solo violins and continuo is followed by *May the god of wit inspire'* with its evocative double echoes. As Titania drifts towards sleep the key changes from C major to C minor, the dance forms disappear, and the music becomes rich and strange. Night sings an ethereal contrapuntal fantasia accompanied only by muted upper strings; Mystery follows with a languorous vocal gavotte; and Secrecy sings the famous *One charming night gives more delight* accompanied by two recorders. Finally, Sleep enters with the command *Hush, no more, be silent all*, and this wonderful scene ends with the Dance for the Followers of Night, a creepy and dissonant double canon inspired by the one in Matthew Locke's music for *The Tempest*, written in 1674.

The music in Act III, an entertainment put on by Titania to charm Bottom, her new-found love, contains *If love's a sweet passion*, one of Purcell's loveliest minuet songs; *Ye gentle spirits of the air*, a spectacular *da capo* number, with a florid declamatory passage enclosing a minuet-like air; and the ever-popular rustic dialogue between Coridon and Mopsa.

Title page of the original printed edition

The masque in Act IV, also conjured up by Titania, ostensibly celebrates Oberon's birthday, though it largely consists of a Masque of the Four Seasons, introduced by Phoebus – an extended metaphor for the renewal of the love between Titania and Oberon. Appropriately, Purcell draws heavily on the idiom of the court ode. It starts with a six-movement symphony, and continues in similar vein, with ground bass airs, and massive choruses. The airs for the four seasons, allocated respectively to soprano, alto, tenor, and bass soloists, are surprisingly intimate, reflective pieces, the first three scored just with pairs of solo obbligato instruments. Winter's air, accompanied throughout by the full spring orchestra, combines the anguished chromatic harmonies of the frost music in *King Arthur* with the grave contrapuntal textures of Night's air in Act II. *The Fairy Queen* ends with the usual masque, put on by Oberon to convince a sceptical Duke Theseus of the potency of magic, and incidentally celebrating love and marriage. Juno appears, 'in a Machine drawn by Peacocks', and sings the brilliant and Italianate *Thrice happy lovers*, and then the scene changes to 'a transparent Prospect of a Chinese Garden, the Architecture, the Trees, the Plants, the Fruits, the Birds, the Beasts quite different to what we have in this part of the World'. However, Purcell made no effort to match this spectacular *chinoiserie* setting with exotic or even rustic music. *Thus the gloomy world* is a superb *da capo* air in Purcell's best Italian manner. But, sung by a Chinaman – whose nation is presumably meant to represent a state of rustic innocence – the piece could not be more incongruous.

Similar things could be said of the parent work. *The Fairy Queen* contains Purcell's most consistently inspired theatre music, yet much of it is devoted to episodes only tangentially connected to the drama, with few dramatic qualities of their own. Also, it cannot be said that the adaptor or adaptors provided Purcell with a wide range of dramatic opportunities, or that Purcell made an effort to provide the range of characters with appropriate musical idioms. He has been praised for finding a special tone for *The Fairy Queen*, a musical equivalent of Shakespeare's *faery*, but it does tend to be applied indiscriminately throughout the work. For this afternoon's performance Richard Andrews has produced a script that provides the context for Purcell's music, and gives a flavour of this strange yet oddly satisfying work, half Shakespeare and half fashionable Restoration spectacle.

Jean-Philippe Rameau (1683-1764)
A Portrait

Portrait of *Rameau* by Carmontelle, 1760

Jean-Philippe Rameau, the greatest French contemporary of Bach and Handel, was born in Dijon on 25 September 1683, the son of a local organist. Little is known of his early life, though his father seems to have taught him music and he made a trip to Milan before being appointed organist of Clermont Cathedral in 1702. In 1706 he was briefly organist of the Collège Louis-le-Grand in Paris before returning to his native city. He remained in the provinces, as organist in Dijon (1709-12), then Lyon (1712-15), and then again at Clermont Cathedral, before finally settling in Paris in 1722. He was to remain there until his death in 1764.

Rameau's motet *Quam dilecta*, a setting of Psalm 84, is

thought to have been written in Lyon, one of three *motets à grand choeur* surviving from that period. It begins with a delicate soprano solo with obbligato flutes, which leads to the vigorous chorus *Cor meum, et caro mea*, an extended and finely worked out double fugue. Then follows the solo *Et enim passer* for *haute-contre* (the characteristically French type of high tenor) in elegant minuet rhythms, again with flute obbligato. After *Altaria tua*, a solemn trio for two sopranos and bass with continuo, the tenor returns with *Beati, qui habitant in domo*, a lively air with chorus. It is followed by *Domine, Deus virtutum*, a reflective solo for *basse-taille* (baritone) with rich orchestral writing. It leads to the final chorus *Domine virtutum*, which consists of a repeated declamatory passage enclosing a section, *Beatus homo*, in dance-like triple time. The other religious work in the programme, *Laboravi clamans*, was published by Rameau in his *Traité de l'harmonie* (1722) as an example of learned counterpoint; much of Rameau's reputation at the time was as a theorist rather than a composer. It is scored for five-part voices and continuo and may have been taken from an otherwise lost motet setting the psalm *Salve me fac Deus*, also written early in his career.

The rest of the programme consists of extracts from Rameau's theatrical music. He did not write his first opera, *Hippolyte et Aricie*, until he was 50, and the one sampled this afternoon, *Les Indes galantes*, was put on in its first version in 1736. It is an example of the *opéra-ballet*, in which dance and operatic music are mixed in self-contained acts or *entrées* linked only by a general overall theme. For this work the theme is love and intrigue in exotic climes, including acts set in South America – *Les Incas de Pérou* – and north America – *Les sauvages*. *Les Incas de Pérou* concerns a love triangle between the Spanish officer Carlos, the Inca princess Phani and the villainous Inca high priest Huascar. In this extract Huascar leads the ceremony of the Adoration of the Sun, consisting of a richly scored sequence of choruses, solos and dances. The ceremony (and our extract) ends suddenly and violently with the eruption of a volcano, engineered by Huascar to disrupt the love between Phani and Carlos. Huascar eventually gets his comeuppance when a rock crushes him during a second eruption. *Les sauvages* also concerns an intrigue between Europeans and Indians, though in this case the 'noble savage' Adario gets the Indian girl Zima. Our extract is the climactic *Danse du grand calumet de paix*, the pipe-smoking ceremony. It is based on a popular harpsichord piece Rameau wrote in 1725, having seen and heard two American Indians performing some of their own dances.

Rameau's next stage work was *Castor et Pollux*, the *tragédie en musique* put on in 1737. In our extract the hero Castor, slain in battle, is in the Elysian Fields. In the air *Séjour de l'eternelle paix* for *haute-contre* and an orchestra of strings, flutes and bassoons he marvels at his surroundings (beautifully evoked by the orchestra), but laments his separation from his beloved, the Princess Telaira. 1739 saw the first performance of *Dardanus* which was later revised in 1744. The famous air *Lieux funestes* comes at the beginning of Act IV in the 1744 version, when Dardanus, also an *haute-contre*, has been taken captive in battle and languishes in prison. His grief is powerfully expressed by biting dissonances and dark orchestral writing coloured by bassoons. The chorus *Chantons tous* comes at the end of the previous act in the 1744 version sung by rejoicing Phrygians. Like the *Danse du grand calumet de paix*, this chorus is a vivid choral and orchestral arrangement of a harpsichord piece, in this case the Tambourin from the third Concert of the *Pièces de clavecin en concerts*, published in 1741.

The other two pieces in the concert come from *actes de ballet* – self-contained one-act works equivalent to an entrée in an *opéra-ballet*. *Pigmalion*, put on in 1748, deals with the sculptor who falls in love with his own creation, brought magically to life by Venus. The *ouverture* is a brilliant representation in music of the sound of Pygmalion's chisel; it was a great favourite at the time as a concert piece. *Les fêtes de Ramire*, produced at Versailles on 22 December 1745, was a reworking by Jean-Jacques Rousseau of numbers from the *comédie-ballet La Princesse de Navarre*, a setting of words by Voltaire. It includes one of Rameau's grandest and most elaborate choral and orchestral chaconnes, more a large-scale rondeau than a set of variations on a ground bass – as in earlier chaconnes. It comes in the final *divertissement* during which Ramire, the son of Alphonse, King of Castile, woos the captive Fatime, Princess of Granada.

Claudio Monteverdi

John Blow

Claudio Monteverdi (1567- 1643)
Il ballo delle ingrate
John Blow (1649-1708)
Venus and Adonis

The two main works in this afternoon's concert, Claudio Monteverdi's *Il ballo delle Ingrate* and John Blow's *Venus and Adonis*, are outstanding examples of the way operatic music and dance were used to adorn and enrich seventeenth-century court culture – and were used to project the power and prestige of the princes who paid for them. *Il ballo* was originally written in Mantua (where Monteverdi was working as *maestro della musica* to Vincenzo I Gonzaga, the Duke of Mantua) and was written as part of the celebrations for the reception in Mantua in June 1608 for Francesco Gonzaga (Vincenzo's eldest son) and his bride Margherita of Savoy after their wedding in Turin. However, the version that has come down to us (in Monteverdi's Eighth Book of Madrigals, 1638), is for a later revival in Vienna; it may have been performed there in December 1636 to celebrate the coronation of Ferdinand III, the new Holy Roman Emperor. There were alterations made to Rinuccini's libretto, with references to Mantua and its River Mincio changed to the German Empire and the Danube, and it is likely that Monteverdi also took the opportunity to modernise the vocal writing.

Throughout his reign Charles II repeatedly tried to establish opera at the Restoration court. He had acquired a taste for it in his years of exile, and it was a potent way of demonstrating that the English were as advanced and sophisticated as other nations. *Venus and Adonis* seems to have been first performed either, in the Hall Theatre at Whitehall Palace on Shrove Tuesday, 19 February 1683 or, later that summer at Windsor Castle in a theatre created in the White Tower. The libretto is by Anne Kingsmill (later Finch), then one of the maids of honour to Mary of Modena, the wife of James, Duke of York – later King James II. We know that Charles II's mistress Mary or Moll Davies played the role of Venus. The nine-year-old Lady Mary Tudor, one of the king's many illegitimate children played the role of Cupid. The other members of the cast were probably drawn from members of the royal music, and one of the recorder players was probably Jacques (or James) Paisible, the French wind player who had arrived in London in 1673 and had married Moll Davies in 1682. In 1684 *Venus and Adonis* was performed again, at the school in Chelsea run by Josiah Priest, famous for putting on Purcell's *Dido and Aeneas* a few years later. There is also a revised version of the work, made in the 1690s perhaps for a concert performance – some of the dances were omitted at that stage.

Il ballo delle Ingrate and *Venus and Adonis* have several features in common, beyond the obvious fact that two of the leading characters are Venus, the goddess of love and her son Amore or Cupid. As we have seen, Blow's Cupid was played by a young girl, but his little Cupids were probably boys from the Chapel Royal, while Monteverdi's Cupid may have been a child of one of the Mantuan court musicians. Rather unusually for the time, Monteverdi wrote the part of Venere – Venus – for an alto singer, though Moll Davies was clearly a conventional soprano. More important, both works depend for their effect on combining dancing – the most essential courtly accomplishment – with a mythological story told in operatic music, in such a way that dance is essential to the plot.

In Monteverdi's *Ballo*, Cupid finds that his arrows have ceased to have their accustomed effect among the court ladies of Mantua (or Vienna in the later version), and so he complains to his mother Venus, who summons Pluto, the god of the underworld. In turn, Pluto (cast as a deep bass as in Monteverdi's opera *Orfeo*) summons up a group of Ingrate – women condemned to Hades for being hard-hearted in love. They dance a grave ballet, accompanied by Monteverdi's beautiful five-part music, and Pluto uses their sad and terrible appearance to reinforce an awful warning to the ladies in the audience. When he orders the Ingrate back to Hades they spring back into action in a much more vigorous and desperate dance, an ingenious set of three variations on a ground bass using respectively the rhythms of the allemande, corrente and gagliarda. Finally, the Ingrate return sadly to Hades, to a strange and halting version of their first dance – with a bar removed from each strain. As they disappear, one of them turns and sings a moving lament for having to leave the 'serene and pure air', echoed by four of her companions.

A.Vivaldi (1678-1741)
G.B.Pergolesi (1710-1736)
Kyrie and *Gloria* & *Missa di San Emidio*

Antonio Vivaldi

The idea for this programme came to me when Andrew Woolley, a former Ph.D. student of mine and now a prominent musicologist specialising in English Baroque music, told me about a manuscript he had discovered in Los Angeles. It was one of Pergolesi's largest-scale and greatest church works, the *Missa di San Emidio* for two choirs and two orchestras; Andrew writes separately about the manuscript and the work below.

Having offered to put on the first performance of his new edition of the mass, I had the idea that it would be interesting to contrast it with sacred works by Pergolesi's great contemporary Antonio Vivaldi. They were both equally famous in the eighteenth century, but for different reasons. Pergolesi's fame rested on his tragically early death (of tuberculosis at the age of 25) after writing two works, the Stabat Mater and the comic opera *La serva padrona*. Vivaldi gained his reputation for developing a type of solo concerto that was also popular all over Europe, influencing J.S. Bach, Handel, Telemann and many others.

Giovanni Battista Pergolesi

Pergolesi and Vivaldi set the mass in similar ways: they both confined themselves to the Kyrie and Gloria, leaving the other movements traditionally set (the 'Credo', 'Sanctus and Agnus Dei') to be provided separately, if at all. This was because they used the structure of the so-called 'cantata mass' in which the texts were divided up into separate movements, mixing choruses and solo arias, and taking much longer to perform than earlier through-composed settings. Vivaldi, like Pergolesi, probably set his 'Kyrie and Gloria' as complete mass settings, but in both cases the corresponding movement has been lost. The Gloria and Kyrie certainly do not belong together. The Gloria is in D major, is for single choir and orchestra with obbligato oboe and trumpet, written around 1715 for the Pietà, the female orphanage in Venice at which Vivaldi taught on-and-off from 1703. The Kyrie dates from at least a decade later, is in G minor, laid out for two choirs and two orchestras without obbligato winds, possibly for performance in a Roman church. As the Pergolesi mass shows (also performed in Rome), the Renaissance practice of separating choirs and orchestras in separate galleries, each with its own organ, was still popular in the city in the eighteenth century.

Vivaldi and Pergolesi also had rather different approaches to their shared musical heritage. Although they both wrote for divided choirs on occasion, Pergolesi's musical idiom is typical of Neapolitan composers in that there is a sharper distinction between the old and new elements. His orchestration is more up-to-date, using horns as well as oboes and trumpets, and the solo arias use the light *galant* style developed in Neapolitan opera in the 1720s, while the choruses often use self-consciously old-fashioned counterpoint, known at the time as the *stile antico*. Vivaldi, by contrast, uses a less polarised, more integrated style, in which choruses and solo arias mostly share a moderately up-to-date idiom. However, Vivaldi uses the *stile antico* in the final movements of both works. In the case of the 'Gloria' we know that the *Cum sancto spiritu* fugue is based on a movement from a setting of the Gloria by the slightly earlier Venetian composer G.M. Ruggieri. The third movement of the 'Kyrie', another *stile antico* fugue, also may be a borrowing, though its model has not been identified.

The two orchestral works are also contrasted in date, style and idiom. Vivaldi was probably the first person to write solo concertos for the violoncello, around 1710. His fine concerto for two violoncellos probably dates from around the same period – a clue being Vivaldi's decision to begin the first movement with just the solo instruments and the continuo. This striking effect he also used in his famous D minor concerto for two solo violins and violoncello, published in 1711 as no. 11 of his op. 3 concerto *L'estro armonico*. As in many of Vivaldi's concertos, the slow movement uses just the soloists with continuo. Pergolesi's sinfonia to his serious opera *L'Olimpiade* written about twenty-five years later, was for a production of the work in Rome in 1735. It is startlingly modern in its orchestration, using horns, trumpets, oboes, strings and continuo, as well as in the style of the first movement, which revels in pure sound and exploits orchestral crescendos – a trick that later became associated with Mannheim composers. It leads to an expressive andante for the strings alone, and then to a formal minuet. Neapolitan sinfonias of this type, detached from their parent operas, became popular in northern Europe (I prepared the edition we are using from manuscripts in Paris and Berlin), and were important models for the later Classical symphony.

Andrew Woolley whose edition we used in this performance provided the following programme note.

Pergolesi wrote two settings of the Kyrie and Gloria (or 'short Mass'), one in D major and another F major, both of which reached their final form by late 1731, or by the end of 1732 at the latest. The F major setting was, like the D major one, conceived originally for a single choir and orchestra. Furthermore, it drew partly upon the D major setting, since the duet for *Domine Deus* was taken from it in largely unaltered form. In almost every other respect, however, the F major setting – as a work for double choir and double orchestra – is considerably grander in both scale and substance. Pergolesi's orchestral conception in the two-choir version is indicated especially by the provision of parts for third and fourth choirs, whose contribution amplifies and elaborates the two-choir structure. In all probability, the double-choir version was written for a performance in Rome at a service in honour of St Emedius, which took place on 31st December 1732 (following an earthquake that struck Naples on 29th November). Another possibility is a performance for an unrecorded occasion after late 1731 connected with another earthquake that happened earlier in 1731 (since it is known that Pergolesi had already written two masses prior to this date). The connection with this particular saint is known because of an inscription at the end of the autograph score of the two-choir version (which the parts for third and fourth choirs supplement), which reads "Finis Laus Deo Beateque Virgini Marie, et Beato Emigdio".

As a whole, the work combines *galant* style solos, a duet and one sextet, with imposing fugal choruses. Striking results are further achieved by harmonic 'special effects', notably in *Qui Tollis* and *Miserere*. Movements tend to form complementary pairs. This is the case for the solo *Laudamus te* and the duet *Domine Deus*, which are both in triple time and in related keys (B minor and E minor). Likewise the two principal fugues, *Christe eleison* and *Gratias agimus tibi* seem perfect demonstrations of how to deploy the rigours of the *stile antico* within an eighteenth century harmonic idiom, in a minor key and a major key respectively (F minor and G major respectively). Cohesion is also achieved through an overall tonal 'arch': following the *Christe eleison*, the piece plunges into D minor at Kyrie II in preparation for the D major *Gloria*. This sets up a 'sharp' key perspective with the return to the tonic major for the final *Cum sancto spiritu* taking place gradually (via B minor, G major, E minor, C minor, and F minor).

The Tuileries – original home of the Concert Spirituel

Concert Spirituel
Music at the French Court

The idea for this programme came when I encountered the last piece, Michel Corrette's extraordinary adaptation of Vivaldi's Spring Concerto, published in Paris in 1766. It was typical of the music performed at the Concert Spirituel, so it seemed a good idea to use this landmark concert series as a peg on which to hang an exploration of the riches of eighteenth-century French sacred music.

I have not confined myself to music performed at the Concert Spirituel since their programmes ranged far beyond French music and religious pieces: the first concert included Corelli's Christmas concerto while it gave the first performance of Mozart's Paris Symphony in 1778 and commissioned Haydn's six Paris symphonies in the 1780s. As always with Leeds Baroque's concert programmes, I have tried to mix in the familiar with the unfamiliar: music by the great composers of the period with their lesser-known contemporaries. I think you will find the pieces by Mondonville, Clérambault and Boismortier equally interesting and entertaining as those by Charpentier, Couperin and Rameau.

The Concert Spirituel, founded in 1725 in a large hall at the Tuileries Palace in Paris, has a special place in the history of French music because it was the beginning of its modern concert life. Until then, the best music was essentially performed in private: at court, in the houses of the nobility, or by the court-sponsored Paris Opéra, the Académie Royale de Musique. Music lovers without court connections had to rely mostly on music performed in church services: Charpentier wrote much of his later music for the Jesuit church in Paris, now known as Saint-Paul Saint-Louis in the Rue Saint Antoine. The function of the Concert Spirituel, a commercial enterprise licensed by the king, was to make available the great repertory of court music to a paying public, something that had begun to happen in England in the 1680s – a measure of how backward French society had become in European terms by the early eighteenth century. It eventually became a highly profitable commercial enterprise, though an umbilical cord connecting it to the court remained. The concerts were held only when the Opéra was closed, most of its directors were still court musicians. These concerts were so associated with the *ancien régime* that it was inevitable that they would come to an end during the Revolution – though the idea of presenting concerts of sacred music during Lent had caught on in other countries, and they were revived in Paris in the nineteenth century.

The principal type of eighteenth-century French sacred music was the *grand motet*. They written mostly for the court chapel, at Versailles or the *chapelle royale* in Paris, they were performed by soloists with a large choir and orchestra. Earlier examples, such as Charpentier's fine setting of Psalm 26, *Dominus illumatio mea* (1699), tend to run sections for the soloists (usually accompanied just by continuo with or without solo violins) into those for the full group without a break. However, by the time Mondonville wrote his *Deus regnavit* (for a concert series in Lille in 1734) it was customary to divide the sections up into separate choral and solo movements. Charpentier's motet is one of his last and most modern works, with eighteenth-century string scoring using two violin parts instead of the old layout with two violas. Mondonville's much more brilliant vocal and instrumental writing featuring solo wind instruments shows how much French music developed in 35 years. In particular, the famous storm chorus *Elevaverunt flumina* (which ensured the motet's popularity at the Concert Spirituel) looks forward to much later music – Haydn's *Creation* comes to mind – in its use of virtuosic choral and orchestral writing to evoke a vivid sound picture of the natural world.

French composers began to modernise their rather archaic musical idiom in the early eighteenth century by importing and imitating Italian music and in particular the concertos of Vivaldi. There are many French Vivaldi imitations and adaptations (including a whole set of sonatas that was accepted as genuine until recently), but none is as bold and memorable as Michel Corrette's setting of Psalm 148, *Laudate Dominum de caelis*, which incorporates Vivaldi's Spring Concerto complete. Corrette (one of Charpentier's successors at the Jesuit church in Paris) had the brilliant insight that Vivaldi's evocation of the natural world in the spring fitted well with the psalmist's contemplation of the variety of God's creation. Thus the storm in Vivaldi's first movement is made to illustrate the words 'fire and hail, snow and vapours, wind and storm'. The slow movement provides barking dogs and serpentine runs to illustrate 'beasts and all cattle, worms and feathered fowls'. The bucolic Pastorale is perfect as an evocation of 'young men and maidens, old men and children'; we can virtually see them dancing in the sunshine. Corrette begins the motet with two movements of his own: an expressive air for solo soprano with obbligato flutes and a prelude featuring the bassoon that serves to introduce Vivaldi's first movement and seems to portray the moment before God's act of creation.

Clérambault, organist of Saint-Sulpice and other churches in Paris, wrote his *Histoire de la Femme Adultère* early in his career: it is listed in a catalogue dated 1724. It is an example of a type of oratorio that goes back to Charpentier and ultimately to Carissimi; Charpentier had studied in Rome and had brought Carissimi's oratorios back to France. Clérambault followed Charpentier in contrasting sections for the protagonists – in this case the Woman taken in Adultery, Jesus, two Jews and a narrator – with passages for the choir and orchestra commenting on the action. Rameau's short contrapuntal setting of *Laboravi clamans*, words from Psalm 69, is also an early work: published in 1722 in his *Traité de l'harmonie* it is an example of elaborate fugal technique. It was probably originally a section for five solo voices of a now-lost *grand motet*, though it makes a fine recital piece for chamber choirs.

In addition to *grands motets*, French eighteenth-century composers wrote *petits motets* for smaller forces, and we include two of them in this concert. François Couperin wrote many of them in his youth, possibly for the court of the exiled James II at Saint-Germain-en-Laye outside Paris, including the expressive setting of the hymn *Salve Regina,* written for the characteristic *haute-contre* or high tenor voice popular in France throughout the eighteenth century. The setting of the hymn *Regina caeli laetare*, published in 1728, is in a later, more Italianate style, using pairs of violins and flutes to accompany the soprano voice. Boismortier had a busy career in Paris as a composer and publisher, producing more than 100 collections of his own music. The instrument *concert* by Lalande comes from a manuscript of *simphonies* said to have been collected in 1737 from material drawn mostly from his operas and ballets and played for the king's suppers over the previous 15 years. An expressive movement with an obbligato bassoon solo leads to a short prelude and then to a lively air.

A Yorkshire weaver

Made in the North –
Provincial Music in the North of England in the Eighteenth and Nineteenth Century

This programme, part of the York Festival of Ideas, celebrates English provincial musical life in the eighteenth and early nineteenth centuries, and particularly in the north of England. We have entitled it *Made in the North* because most of the composers were born there and in some cases spent their entire working lives there, and because some of them were drawn from the artisan classes – men otherwise occupied by making things in northern England's developing industrial revolution. Some of them, such as the weaver Edward Harwood, the house painter Richard Taylor or the cobbler Thomas Clark, were Sunday composers, though the Rev John Pixell was presumably busy on Sundays – a Monday composer, perhaps. Some of the more ambitious eventually earned their living from music: Harwood became a noted alto singer in Liverpool and Taylor a music seller in Chester. Some composers, such as John Alcock of Lichfield or Charles Avison of Newcastle, were provincial organists who spent much of their time writing for local groups. Others, such as William Shield from near Gateshead, Edmund Ayrton from Ripon or James Nares from York, eventually made it in the London musical scene. We end the concert with a piece by Handel because he was performed all over the country, and his choral style was the starting-point for most northern composers far into the nineteenth century.

Much of the music in the programme was written for Church of England parish churches or dissenting chapels. The repertory developed as part of an early eighteenth-century movement to revitalise parish worship, with the formation of Church and Chapel choirs. In time this distinctive repertory of metrical psalms and hymns, often in simple block chords, as in Taylor's *Crucifixion* with its rich, dissonant harmony, or his *Resurrection*, which is in the more elaborate 'fuguing tune' style with a section of counterpoint established itself. At first the choirs performing this repertory sang unaccompanied, though around 1800 they were increasingly accompanied by groups of instruments; most rural parish churches at the time did not have organs. One of the most famous fuguing tunes is *Cranbrook*, by the Canterbury composer Thomas Clark. We have included it because it was very popular in northern England. It became associated with the Christmas hymn 'While shepherds watched', and eventually became the tune *for On Ilkla Moor baht 'at* – making Clark an honorary Yorkshireman!

By the early nineteenth century some provincial composers were writing psalm settings with elaborate orchestral accompaniment, probably for choral festivals. A good example is John Foster's setting of Psalm 50 in the 'old version' of Sternhold and Hopkins, fully scored for choir with two flutes and strings. Foster came from a higher social class than most psalmody composers: he was a landowner and JP from near Sheffield. Some of the psalmody repertory consists of adaptations of instrumental music, a case in point being Sir John Stevenson's use of a movement from a concerto by Charles Avison to set Thomas Moore's poetic version of Miriam's Song from the Book of Exodus. Provincial composers sometimes chose highbrow religious poetry, as in Edward Harwood's setting of *Vital spark of heavn'ly flame*, Alexander Pope's poem *The Dying Christian to his Soul*. It is remarkably sophisticated and up-to-date for a provincial composer of the 1760s, using the 'sensibility' style coming into

England from Germany. John Pixell's *When rising from the bed of death* is a fine setting of Joseph Addison's *A Thought in Sickness*. It belongs to a tradition of orchestral songs much cultivated in the midlands; Pixell was vicar of Edgbaston near Birmingham.

Northern professional composers also tended to cultivate genres current in London. James Nares's *Call to remembrance* is a fine example of the type of full-with-verse anthem cultivated by cathedral composers ever since Purcell's time, in which contrapuntal full sections are contrasted with brief solos. Nares was organist of York Minster from 1735 to 1756, when he returned to London to become one of the organists of the Chapel Royal. Edmund Ayrton from Ripon was a pupil of Nares at York and eventually joined him in the Chapel Royal. His anthem *Begin unto my song with timbrels* is scored for full orchestra, but we are performing two extracts using reduced forces, as often happened in the provinces at the time; the whole work is found in cut-down form in a manuscript now in the Brotherton Library at the University of Leeds. Ayrton's style is essentially Handelian, but with a distinctive local accent. His models would have been pieces such as Handel's four coronation anthems, written in 1727 for George II. 'Let thy hand be strengthened' is the only one of the four not to require trumpets and drums. William Shield's *My God, my King* is an example of the refined setting of metrical psalms popular in London. It consists of a soprano solo accompanied by a violoncello followed by a full section in which in the women's and men's voices of the choir are contrasted and combined in sophisticated ways. Shield came from a village near Gateshead and worked in Scarborough, Newcastle and Durham before coming to London.

Provincial organists were also often involved in running concerts in their towns and cities, using orchestras made up of a nucleus of local professional instrumentalists (often drawn from the municipal waits) and gentlemen amateurs drawn from the surrounding area. As these orchestral societies developed in the 1730s and 40s it was quickly realised that the repertory of *concerti grossi* derived from Corelli and used by Geminiani, Handel and other London composers was ideal for their purposes. Professionals could take the difficult solo violin and violoncello parts while the 'gentlemen' played the easier but still satisfying orchestral parts. Charles Avison wrote many concertos of this sort for the Newcastle Musical Society, which he ran from the 1730s, and in 1744 he published a set of ingenious concerto arrangements of Domenico Scarlatti's harpsichord sonatas, then becoming popular in England. Italian composers were popular in the north east: the Durham composer John Garth published English versions of the famous psalm settings by the Venetian composer Benedetto Marcello, and included his *In omnem terram,* an ingenious six-part triple canon. John Alcock published his set of concertos in 1750, the year he became organist of Lichfield cathedral. It uses the Corelli format, though with two flute parts in addition to the solo violins, an innovation copied from Geminiani. Flutes were the only wind instrument considered suitable for gentlemen to play at the time.

A concerto performance by Leeds Baroque directed by Peter Holman

The Baroque Concerto:
Corelli, Vivaldi and Handel

2013 is the 300th anniversary of the death of Arcangelo Corelli, so we open this programme with the seventh of his twelve concerti grossi op. 6, published shortly after his death. It is not known exactly when it (or any of the other concertos in the set) was composed, though its style suggests that it is one of the earlier ones, perhaps written in the 1680s. In particular, there are places in the second section where the *concertino* (two solo violins, solo violoncello and harpsichord continuo) and the *concerto grosso* (the orchestra with organ continuo) operate as two separate groups as in earlier double-choir works; in most of Corelli's concertos the *concertino* plays throughout, with the *concerto grosso* entering from time to time to reinforce it.

By the time Vivaldi's op. 10 concertos were published, in Amsterdam in 1729, the standard form of the concerto had changed from a patchwork of short contrasted sections, as in Corelli, to three sizeable movements, in the pattern fast-slow-fast. It was also now more common for concertos to feature a single solo instrument, and for it to be a wind instrument rather than the violin. Vivaldi's op. 10 was the first set of flute concertos to be published, and brings together six works written at various times, some of which were originally for recorder. In the fast movements of no. 4, *Il gardellino*, the flute imitates the song of the goldfinch with chirping repeated notes and the rapid alternation of notes a fourth apart. The slow movement is a soulful melody in the style of a Venetian gondola song accompanied just by the continuo.

Handel's twelve *concerti grossi* op. 6 (or 'grand concertos', as they were called when they were published) were written at high speed in the autumn of 1739. They were evidently written to be performed as interval music during performances of his oratorios in the 1739-40 season, though it is clear that he also planned to publish them as a set. Collaborating with the publisher John Walsh the younger, Handel had issued his organ concertos op. 4 the previous year, and a set of trio sonatas op. 5 earlier in 1739. By numbering his concertos op. 6 Handel was referring to Corelli's *concerti grossi* op. 6, the set that achieved classic status throughout Europe in the early eighteenth century. No. 11 is one of the finest of the set, with beautiful writing for the solo strings; it comes as a shock to find that it seems to be an arrangement of an organ concerto. Of the four main movements, the first features birdsong imitations while having something of the character of the first movement of a French overture; the second movement is the expected fugue. The last two are large-scale and highly sophisticated movements in aria form, the first in the rhythm of a slow minuet, the second a vigorous dance in duple time but with something of the character of a triple-time hornpipe.

Leeds Baroque repertoire 2000-2018

June 2000 St. Chad's, Headingley
G.F. Handel: *Messiah*, with Philippa Hyde (soprano), Robert Ogden (countertenor) and Mark Rowlinson (bass)

October 2000 St Wilfrid's Church, Harrogate
A Tribute to J.S. Bach – Motets by Bach interspersed, with organ music played by Graham Barber

November 2000
From Corelli to Mozart: A Century of the Baroque Concerto, with Crispian Steele-Perkins, (natural trumpet) and Duncan Druce (Baroque viola) – Concertos by Corelli, Muffat, Festing, J.S. Bach, Michael Haydn and Mozart

March 2000
G.F. Handel: *Acis and Galatea,* with Philippa Hyde (soprano), Rupert Jennings (tenor) and Adrian Peacock (bass)

April 2001
Arne: *The Judgment of Paris*, with Leeds University Project Choir

May 2001 Toll Gavel Methodist Church (Beverley Early Music Festival)
Arne: *The Judgment of Paris*

(Conference: *English Music in the Provinces* by Leeds University Centre for English Music)
Ye people all with one accord – Orchestral music and anthems by North Country composers 1750-1850

October 2001
Carissimi and Monteverdi – Monteverdi choral and solo pieces and Carissimi: *Jephte*

November 2001
Bach in the Great Hall – J.S. Bach: *Sanctus* in D, Cantatas 58 and 140, 2 motets and double violin concerto, with Philippa Hyde (soprano) and Tassilo Erhard (violin)

February 2002
Purcell: *King Arthur*, with Leeds University Project choir and Rebecca Saunders (soprano), Adrian Peacock (bass), Jane Oakshott and Peter Meredith (narrators)

May 2002
Music for the Pietà – Cantatas and concertos by Vivaldi, with Lawrence Zazzo (countertenor), George Kennaway (cello), and Rachel Latham (flute)

June 2002
Gentlemen of the Chapel Royal – Sacred music by Tallis, Byrd, Tomkins, Gibbons, Blow, Purcell etc., with Richard Rastall and Peter Meredith (readers)

September 2002 Castle Howard (Charity concert for MIND)
Orchestral pieces by Telemann, Corelli, Vivaldi and Mozart

Music for Shakespeare – Vocal and instrumental music for Shakespeare's plays (LUCEM)

November 2002
G.F. Handel: *Israel in Egypt,* with Leeds University Project Choir

March 2003 St Chad's Headingley and Halifax Parish Church
J.S. Bach: *St John Passion,* with Philippa Hyde (soprano), Lawrence Zazzo (countertenor) and Mark Rowlinson (bass)

May 2003
Mozart and his World – Works by J.C. Bach, C.P.E. Bach, Mozart, W.F. Bach and Haydn, with Catherine Hopper (soprano), Jennifer Hardy (cello) and Rachel Latham (flute)

July 2003 Music in 19C Britain Conference
Music for a city set on a hill – Music by Latrobe

November 2003
Mozart/Wilby: *Mass in C minor* (1st Performance), with Leeds University Project Choir, and Plainsong Choir of the College of the Resurrection, Mirfield

February 2004
Handel: *Esther,* with Philippa Hyde (soprano) and James Griffett (tenor)

April 2004 Classical Association of England and Wales Conference
Latin Poetry in Renaissance and Baroque Music – Music by Arne, Josquin, Willaert, Arcadelt, Lassus, de Rore etc.

June 2004
Music for London's Pleasure Gardens – Works by Lindley, Boyce, Arne, Handel, Sammartini, Dibdin and Lampe

November 2004 Heinrich Biber Anniversary Concert
Biber: *Missa Salisburgensis* a 56, with York Waits, Quintessential and Crispian Steele-Perkins (trumpet) and Leeds University Project Choir

February 2005
Handel: *L'allegro, il Penseroso ed il Moderato,* with Philippa Hyde and Nicola Mills (sopranos)

June 2005
J.S. Bach and the Concerto, with Gail Henessey (oboe) and Francisco del Amo (viola da gamba)

October 2005
Schütz: *Musikalische Exequien* and *Deutsches Magnificat,* with Graham Barber (organ)

November 2005
J.S. Bach: *St Matthew Passion*, with Philippa Hyde (soprano), Stephen Varcoe (bass) and Leeds University Project Choir

December 2005
Charpentier: *Messe de Minuit*

March 2006
Henry Purcell: *The Fairy Queen,* with Philippa Hyde (soprano), Philip Smith (baritone), Crispian Steele-Perkins (natural trumpet), Jane Oakshott and Peter Meredith (narrators)

June 2006
'*Le Grand Siècle*' – French Baroque orchestral music, with Rachel Latham (flute)

November 2006
J.S. Bach: *Mass in B Minor*, with Nicola Mills (soprano), Philip Smith (bass) and Leeds University Project Choir

February 2007
Handel: *Alexander's Feast,* with Philippa Hyde (soprano) and Philip Smith (bass)

June 2007 Theatre Royal, Richmond, North Yorkshire
Water Music – Works by Telemann, Vivaldi, de Lalande and Handel

Temple Newsam House, Leeds
Court, City, Country: A Seventeenth-Century Musical Tour of Britain – Music by Gibbons, Tomkins, Byrd, Dering, Ravenscroft etc.
November 2007
Restoration Odes – Works including Henry Purcell: *Come ye sons of art, away*; Giovanni Battista Draghi: *From Harmony, heavenly harmony;* Jeremiah Clarke: *Pay your thanks* and *Tell the world*

March 2008
A Portrait of Charpentier – including *Te Deum*, *Canticum pro pace* and *Magnificat* in D minor, with the Leeds University Project Choir

June 2008 Theatre Royal, Richmond, North Yorkshire
The Lass of Richmond Hill – Music for the Georgian theatre by Arne, Boyce, Stanley, Dibdin and Hook, with Philippa Hyde (soprano) and Rachel Latham (flute)

November 2008
Handel*: Messiah*

March 2009
Handel in Italy – Orchestral music by Handel, Corelli and Pergolesi

May 2009 Grinton Parish Church (Swaledale Festival)
In the Voice of Praise and Thanksgiving – A concert of English Baroque sacred music, with works by Croft, Purcell, Blow, Boyce, Handel etc.

June 2009
Purcell and Handel: An Anniversary Celebration – including Purcell: *Praise the Lord, O Jerusalem* and Handel: *As Pants the Hart* and *Dixit Dominus*

November 2009 Haydn Anniversary concert
Haydn: *The Creation,* with Leeds University Project Choir

February 2010
J.S. Bach: *Magnificat* in D, *Ascension Oratorio* (Cantata 11) and Cantata 34, with Philip Smith (baritone)

March 2010 Leeds Baroque 10th Anniversary Concert, Salt's Mill, Saltaire
Purcell: *The Indian Queen*, with Crispian Steele-Perkins (trumpet), Philip Smith (baritone) and Jack Edwards (reader)

October 2010
Vivaldi: *Venetian Vespers* and Porpora: *Dixit Dominus* in G

November 2010 Leeds Cathedral
Monteverdi: *Vespers* (1610), liturgical reconstruction for the Feast of the Presentation, with Leeds University Project Choir

February 2011 (Northern Premiere performance)
C.P.E. Bach: *St Matthew Passion*

April 2011 Collaboration with Bradford Chorale
The Glories of Venice – Monteverdi, Gabrieli and Vivaldi

June 2011
Scenes from Molière – Music for the theatre by Lully and Charpentier

October 2011
Mozart in Salzburg – Works including *Coronation Mass, Exsultate jubilate, Litaniae de venerabili* and *Serenata notturna,* with Sarah Potter (soprano)

February 2012
Music for State Occasions – Music by Locke, Blow, Purcell, Croft and Handel

June 2012 Theatre Royal, Richmond North Yorkshire
A Day of Rare Treats – Music from the North East in the Eighteenth Century, with George Kennaway (cello)

October 2012
Henry Purcell: *Dioclesian*, with Crispian Steele-Perkins (trumpet)

March 2013
G.F. Handel: *Israel in Egypt,* with the Leeds University Project Choir

May 2013 Holy Trinity Church, Skipton
Sacred and Profane – Music including Carissimi: *Jephte* and Charpentier: *Acteon*, with Daniel Auchincloss (tenor/haute-contre)

June 2013
Flute concerti by Handel and Vivaldi, and J.S. Bach cantatas Nos. 82 and 209, with Rachel Latham (flute)

October 2013
Madrigals of Love and War – A programme of Monteverdi madrigals with continuo

Music to celebrate the signing of the Treaty of Utrecht
Handel *Te Deum* and *Jubilate* in D, Croft: *With Noise of Cannon*, with James Laing (countertenor)

March 2014 (Special alumni concert)
J.S. Bach: *Mass in B Minor*

June 2014 United Reform Church, Saltaire, supported by The Early Music Shop
Purcell: *Dido and Aeneas*, with Sarah Potter (soprano)

October 2014 Collaboration, with the School of Music, University of Huddersfield
A Bach-Abel Concert: Early classical soprano arias, symphonies and concertos by J.C. Bach, Abel, Stamitz and the young Mozart, with Sarah Potter (soprano) and Samuel Stadlen (viola da gamba)

December 2014
J.S. Bach at Christmas – *Nun komm der heiden Heiland* BWV61, *Sanctus* in *D* BWV238, *Es ist ein Kind geboren* BWV142, *Mass in A major* BWV23 and *Ehre sei dir, Gott* (*Christmas Oratorio*, Part 5) BWV248/5

March 2015
Gloria! Sacred Music by Pergolesi and Vivaldi – Pergolesi: *Messa di San Emidio* (*Missa Romana*) in F, Sinfonia to *L'Olimpiade* and Antonio Vivaldi: Concerto in G minor RV531, *Kyrie* in G minor RV587 and *Gloria* in D RV589.

June 2015
Purcell: *King Arthur* (or *The British Worthy*), with Richard Andrews (narrator)

November 2015
Handel's Music for State Occasions including *Zadok the Priest*, *This is the Day*, and the first performance of a specially-commissioned work for Leeds Baroque by Christopher Roberts

February 2016 Leeds Early Music Festival
Concert Spirituel – Motets by Couperin, Rameau, Mondonville and Boismortier, featuring Corrette: *Laudate Dominum*, with Philippa Hyde (soprano), Daniel Auchincloss (haute-contre) and Asuka Sumi (violin)

June 2016
Claudio Monteverdi: *Il ballo delle Ingrate* and John Blow: *Venus and Adonis*, with Richard Wistreich (bass)

November 2016
Howard Assembly Room, Leeds (Birthday concert for Peter Holman)
A Portrait of Heinrich Biber – Sonata no. 12 in C (*Sonatae tam aris*), *Missa Sancti Henrici*, Sonata no. 10 in G minor, Offertory Motet: *In sole posuisti*, Communion Motet: *Litaniae Laurentanae*, Partita no. 3 in A, *Battalia* (*Sonate di Marche*) in D and Serenada a5 in C, *Der Nachtwächter*

March 2017
Young Mendelssohn and Mozart – Mendelssohn: *Aus tiefer Noth schrei' ich zu dir*, *Salve Regina*, *Christe du Lamm Gottes*, *Ave Maria*, op. 23, no. 2 and *Wer nur den lieben Gott laβt walten*; Mozart, completed Druce: *Requiem in D minor* K626, with Leeds University Project Choir

June 2017
National Centre for Early Music (for the York Festival of Ideas)
Made in the North – A celebration of the music composed, published or performed in the North of England during the eighteenth century, with works by Edmund Ayrton of Ripon, Charles Avison of Newcastle, Edward Harwood of Liverpool, Thomas Clark of Canterbury, John Foster of High Green, James Nares, William Shield, John Alcock of Lichfield, Richard Taylor of Chester and Handel

October 2017:
Friends & Rivals Johann Sebastian Bach & Georg Philipp Telemann – Bach: *Actus Tragicus* BWV 106, *Christ lag in Todesbanden* BWV 4 and Violin concerto in G minor BWV 1056; Telemann: Concerto for recorder and flute and *Ach wie nichtig, ach, wie flüchtig*

March 2018
A Portrait of Jean-Philippe Rameau – Grand motet *Quam dilecta*, Overture to *Pigmalion*, solos from *Dardanus* and *Castor et Pollux*, chaconne from *Les fêtes de Ramire* and extracts from *Les Indes galantes,* with Nicholas Sales (haute-contre)

June 2018
Henry Purcell: *The Fairy Queen*, with Richard Andrews (narrator)

October 2018 The Venue, Leeds College of Music
Handel: *L'Allegro, il Penseroso ed il Moderato*, with Judit Felszeghy (soprano) and Richard Robbins (tenor)

www.ingramcontent.com/pod-product-compliance
Lightning Source LLC
Chambersburg PA
CBHW041429190426
43193CB00050B/2987